A Half Acre of Hell

Lt. Avis Dagit, 1942

Kitty
Best wishes to a
sister nurse
Avis D. Schorer

A Half Acre
of Hell

A Combat Nurse in WW II

Avis D. Schorer

2000
Galde Press, Inc.
Lakeville, Minnesota, U.S.A.

A Half Acre of Hell
© Copyright 2000 by Avis D. Schorer
All rights reserved.
Printed in the United States of America
No part of this book may be used or reproduced in any manner whatsoever
without written permission from the publishers except in the case of brief
quotations embodied in critical articles and reviews.

First Edition
First Printing, 2000

Library of Congress Cataloging-in-Publication Data
Schorer, Avis D.
    A half acre of hell : a combat nurse in WW II / Avis D. Schorer.
        p.   cm.
    ISBN 1–880090–94–5 (trade pbk.)
        1. Schorer, Avis D.   2. World War, 1939–1945—Personal narratives,
American.   3. United States Army—Nurses—Biography.   4. World War,
1939–1945—Campaigns—Italy.   5. Anzio Beachhead, 1944—Personal
narratives, American.   I. Title.

D811.5 .S3448 2000
940.54'7573'092—dc21   00–041704

Galde Press, Inc.
PO Box 460
Lakeville, Minnesota 55044–0460

Contents

Acknowledgments

I HAD PUSHED THE MEMORIES of my days as an army nurse during World War II to the back of my mind. After my children were raised and I retired as a Nurse Anesthetist, I tried to read about other nurses in the war and found that little had been written. My children encouraged me to write of my experiences.

First of all, I want to thank William B. Breuer, who graciously wrote the foreword to this book. Mr. Breuer is a well-known author and important historian of World War II. He has written many books covering almost every phase of the war. I appreciate his generosity and counsel.

I am unable to express adequate thanks to the wonderful members of the Augsburg Park Library Writers Group: Alice Vollmar, Dick Graber, Jan Graber, Mary Culhane, Ena Cordes, Janet Johnson, Judy Peacock, Fran Klette, Maureen Fischer, and Karol Toso. I reserve special thanks for Bonnie Graves, who has counselled and given support beyond measure. Without the help of these people, this book could not have been written.

I am glad that a few members of the 56th Evacuation Hospital had the foresight to write a history of the hospital. Their record of times, statistics, and places makes the book historically accurate.

Special thanks to Phyllis Galde and her staff at Galde Press for their expertise and suggestions in producing this book.

A big thank you goes to my children, Anna, Joseph, and John for their love and encouragement every step of the way. When my grandchildren study World War II, they will have a better understanding of what Grandma did during the war. I am grateful that John introduced me to computers and word processing, which made writing a less daunting task.

Foreword

ALTHOUGH OFFICIALLY LISTED as noncombatants, United States Army nurses in World War II often found themselves in extreme peril because of the shifting tides of battles. One of the most remarkable of these instances occurred in January 1944 when an American and British force of 70,000 soldiers stormed ashore far behind German lines at Anzio, a small fishing port on the west coast of Italy.

That invasion set the stage for one of the most brutal and bizarre armed conflicts that history has known—and some 230 U.S. Army female nurses, including the author of this book, were trapped with the fighting men on a narrow strip of Italian flatland 18 miles long and only four to seven miles deep.

Famed Civil War General William Sherman immortalized the expression, "War is hell!" but he never knew the half of it. Sherman had never been in the Devil's Cauldron of Anzio.

The Allied plan called for a rapid buildup of supplies and equipment on the Anzio beachhead, then a lightning-like thrust northward for 30 miles to capture the glittering prize of Rome. However, the German commander in Italy reacted to the invasion with typical Teutonic speed and skill. Within 72 hours he ringed the bridgehead with scores of tanks and first-rate troops.

On D-Day plus 5 the author, then Lieutenant Avis Dagit of the U.S. Army Nurse Corps, and other members of her evacuation hospital landed under a hail of German bombs and artillery shells. Along the shoreline, the medical people began attending to a floor of wounded men in a collection of tents that rapidly gained the ominous sobriquet Hell's Half Acre.

So crowded was the Allied-held terrain that the hospital was located next to supply depots, ammunition dumps, various headquarters, and other prime German targets, resulting in bombs and shells crashing around and onto the tented hospital.

Anzio was a clash of steel wills. Adolf Hitler demanded that the hostile beachhead be destroyed at all costs. Allied leaders ordered the enclave to be held to the last man, if need be.

A German radio propagandist known to the Americans as the Berlin Bitch called the bridgehead "the world's largest self-contained prisoner of war camp."

Perched on the surrounding heights, Germans with high powered binoculars and range finders looked down on every move on the beachhead. A torrent of shells exploded almost ceaselessly, day and night. There was no such thing as a "rear area." Some days it was worse on the front lines, other times the danger was more acute on Hell's Half Acre.

The brutalities and rigors of Anzio would be forever seared in each survivor's brain as if from a blow torch. Lieutenant Dagit and the other army nurses endured the interminable days and nights. Their handmaidens were death, doom and disaster.

In her lively writing style the author takes the reader into the horrors—and heroism—of Hell's Half Acre. Conditions were almost unbearable, as the nurses, without complaint, toiled ceaselessly to save the lives and relieve the suffering of their hideously mutilated patients.

While wearing steel helmets, fatigues, and combat boots, the nurses would perform their duties for as long as 36 hours without food or sleep. Often they heard the frightening rustle of a 700-pound shell fired from what the Allies called the Anzio Express, an enormous railroad gun, just before a ground-shaking blast erupted nearby.

At night German airplanes flew low along the shore, dropped parachute flares to light targets, then unloaded their bombs.

On occasion wounded men lying on cots in the tented hospital received clusters to their Purple Hearts when they were hit again by shell or bomb fragments. During these bombardments the lady nurses refused to abandon their patients and take cover.

The presence of the nurses in the Anzio inferno served as a gigantic morale booster for the fighting men at a time when it seemed almost certain that the Germans would wipe out the bridgehead. So inspiring was the valor displayed by the women that an attitude emerged among the troops: "If they can take it, so can I!"

After being trapped for nearly three months, the Allies broke out of the beachhead and captured Rome. Victory in war is never cheap: Thousands of American and British troops had been killed or wounded. At Hell's Half Acre, the nurses also paid a heavy price. Bombs and shells killed six of the women and wounded 16 others.

Four nurses were awarded Silver Stars, the first American women to earn that coveted decoration for valor.

This excellent book is a glowing tribute, not only to the valiant nurses who had endured without flinching the horrors of Anzio, but also to military nurses around the world whose devotion to duty helped preserve American freedoms in World War II.

WILLIAM B. BREUER
Combat veteran and author of thirty nonfiction books

Chapter I

Induction

All branches of the military service need nurses," said Miss Wesslund. "If they don't get enough volunteers, they will draft nurses. You're young and aren't married. There is no reason why you can't volunteer." Her threat of a few days earlier still burned in my mind when I awoke on September 12, 1941. It was my last day as a student nurse at Iowa Methodist Hospital in Des Moines, Iowa.

I went to bed early the night before so I would be ready for my big day. Janey, my roommate, finished training a few days earlier. Her empty bed gave me a place to arrange my student uniform for the last time. No more starched bibs and aprons over blue-and-white-striped dresses. I removed the two narrow black-velvet bands on my cap and put it on the lamp. Tomorrow, a white uniform and wide black band on my cap would show that I was a graduate nurse. A little shudder of excitement ran down my spine. The cool, marble window sill was a perfect place to keep the corsage from my family fresh until morning. I went to bed and dreamed of a bright future.

1

I hurried to the cafeteria for morning chapel services. I reached the door a few minutes before it closed on the heels of the last student nurse. After three years of mandatory chapel attendance, this one had special meaning. All eyes turned toward me when we sang "God Be With You Until We Meet Again." The student body sang the hymn in honor of my graduation. I swallowed hard and blinked back tears that blurred the faces of my friends. The traditional song never had so much meaning. Pressures mounted and several of my classmates already planned to enter military service.

The storm clouds of war in Europe grew darker each day. Young men registered for the draft and many left for the service every day. The news about the war in Europe had a chilling effect on everyone. It tore families apart. A few postponed their college education. Others married hastily to avoid the draft. We did not allow ourselves to think of fighting this war. It was in far-off Europe.

"What do you plan to do now, Avis?" Helen asked as we walked slowly to the elevator that took us to the sixth floor.

"Miss Jones offered me a job here for sixty-five dollars a month. It'll be enough money for me to rent an apartment with Bette, Midge, and Maribelle," I said. "We found a two-bedroom apartment just two blocks from the hospital. My share of the rent will be two-fifty per week. What are your plans?"

"After I write State Boards and see the results," Helen said, "I'll decide if I should join the navy. The salary they're offering here sounds good compared to the thirty-five dollars per month nurses were making a few years ago."

"I want to repay the folks the money they spent on my schooling," I said. "I'll enjoy a paycheck. I hope I'll have a little left for new clothes."

The elevator stopped at the sixth floor and we left for our duty stations.

I was busy preparing the medicine tray when the supervisor appeared in the doorway.

"Miss Wesslund wants to see you in the training school office," she said. "I'll have someone else finish the tray."

Since I was no longer a student nurse, what could she want to see me about? The door was open and I walked across the dreaded "green carpet" to her desk. A troubled look clouded her face and her brown eyes were softer than I remembered them.

"Congratulations, Miss Dagit." Before I could offer my thanks, she asked, "Do you plan to go into the service? You know these young men need someone to care for them."

"I have…haven't decided," I stammered.

"Do you want to be drafted? If you sign up now, you'll have a choice."

"I'll think about it." I felt trapped. How could I escape?

I was off the following Saturday afternoon and Sunday morning and that gave me enough time to go home and talk to the folks about the idea.

We gathered around the supper table—Mother, Dad, and seven of my brothers and sisters. I took a deep breath and said, "Miss Wesslund thinks I should join the service."

Dad replied without looking up from his plate, "And why would you want to do that?"

Mother's voice did not conceal her concern. She replied, "Oh, I hope you won't. Uncle Adolph always had poor health after he spent a year in New Mexico during World War I. You have a good job there in Des Moines. Leona works and lives near by." I tried to understand her reasoning. My sister, Leona, and I were in the same class at school and were very close.

After our brief discussion, I decided to return to Des Moines. I would work well into the future at Iowa Methodist Hospital despite all the changes in the world.

A recruiter from the Red Cross came to the hospital in late November. All the nurses at the hospital attended her presentation. She gave us the positive aspects of joining the Red Cross. She appealed to our spirit of adventure, patriotism, and romance.

"You will be called to serve only if there is a national emergency," she said. "In that case, you'll receive all subsistence and be paid seventy dollars per month. And by the way, statistics show that seventy-five percent of nurses meet their husbands while in the army or navy."

Everyone received application blanks for the Red Cross. Two of the questions were, "In a National Emergency, would you be willing to serve?" and the other, "In which branch of the service would you serve?" My answers were "yes" to the first question and to the second question "army."

I made plans to go home the next weekend and tell the family of my decision.

Very little good news came from Europe in the days ahead. Dad, especially, thought we should stay out of any conflict outside our own country. I again waited until the supper hour before breaking the news that I had joined the Red Cross. I was acutely aware of the worried look that crossed Mother's face as I spoke.

"Oh, don't worry. They won't call me unless we're at war. If that happens, I'd make it clear I'll only serve one year."

The results of the State Boards came through in record time and everyone in our class passed them. Maribelle decided to return to Grand Junction. Midge moved with her family to Bremerton, Washington. Bette planned to take an extended vacation, a luxury I could not afford.

"I hate to do this to you, Avis, because you probably won't want to keep this apartment alone," said Bette. There was a tinge of concern in her voice.

"Don't worry about me," I replied. "Shirley and Judy downstairs invited me to move in with them. They both plan to stay in Des Moines and find work when they finish Business School." I tried to hide the disappointment I felt because of my roommates leaving before I had firm plans of my own.

Next morning was December 7, 1941, and I was up early to pack for my move downstairs. The day was gray, typical for Des Moines in December. The temperature was above freezing and we didn't have snow. I thought momentarily that I should go to church and then dismissed the idea. I had to be out of the apartment by the end of the week. I gathered the student nurse's uniforms in one box to send home. I found another box for the three year's accumulation of textbooks. I started to remove the books from the shelves that flanked the fireplace when I heard a knock at the door. Before I could cross the room, the door burst open. It was Phil from downstairs. His face was ashen.

"Turn on the radio!" he shouted. "Japan bombed Pearl Harbor! President Roosevelt just announced we declared war on Japan!"

I was momentarily speechless. "Why Japan and where is Pearl Harbor?" I finally managed to say, still unable to grasp the enormity of what he was saying.

We had heard only about Hitler's conquests and the war in Europe. My heart pounded and I felt the blood drain from my face. Despite the static on the radio, we heard President Roosevelt tell us, "The Japanese carried out a sneak bombing attack early this morning. There are many thousand casualties, both killed and wounded." The shocking news seared our minds. We wanted to do something, but fear of what lay ahead paralyzed us. A few days later, he declared, "This day will live in infamy."

I knew there was a chance I might be in the service when I joined the Red Cross. A choking realization struck that I'd be on active duty; the President said we were at war. Through the dark days of the Depression, I heard President Roosevelt assure us the days ahead would be better. Now he was telling us we were at war! Conflicting reports about the number of killed and wounded filled the airwaves. Each report was worse than the last. I wanted to run home and talk to Mother and Dad. I felt an overwhelming need for the security of family and home. Deep down, I knew our lives had changed on December 7.

It was less than an hour before I reported for work. I grabbed my coat and ran down the two flights of stairs to the street. I half ran to the hospital as thoughts rushed through my mind. What would happen to my brothers and friends and, yes, to me? There were others at the hospital to talk with and I needed to talk with someone. I sensed the shock everyone felt when I walked through the front door. All the security I had known here for the past three years had suddenly vanished. We gathered in the cafeteria, hall, and medicine room. We talked about who would leave for military service and who would care for those at home.

The United States declared war with Germany on December 11, 1941.

Anguished and confused thoughts crowded my mind following Pearl Harbor. It was hard to think about the Christmas holidays. I had a paycheck for the first time and this year, more than ever, I wanted to buy each member of my family a Christmas gift. I walked down the hill toward downtown to shop. The carols from the tower of the Equitable Life building took on a whole new meaning. How long would it be before we knew, "Peace on earth and good will toward men?"

I received my first communication from "Uncle Sam" just before Christmas. The orders read: "Report to Fort Des Moines in Des Moines, Iowa, for a physical examination on December 20, 1941."

Leona took the day off to accompany me on this lonely and frightening trip to the fort. It was a gray, chilly day. We took the streetcar to the end of the line on the edge of the city. We transferred to another car that went only to the fort.

The low, red-brick buildings, forgotten for many years, were alive with activity. Soldiers marched on the parade grounds. Tanks, army vehicles, and guns filled a large field. Men in Jeeps scurried everywhere. Without a doubt, we were truly at war.

The physical exam was thorough. I answered an endless number of questions about my past and present health.

"I'm going to send you to Room 302 and have Captain Blair examine you," said the examining officer. "I've found a weakness in your abdominal wall. You may have a hernia."

How could this be? I had always been such a healthy person. I then realized that I wanted to join the service. Since many of my classmates were in the army or navy, I wanted to join them.

I heard from the army after Christmas. I had passed the physical exam and further orders would follow. I resigned my job and went home to spend time with the family before I reported for active duty.

The recruiter told us to say where we would like to report. They tried to send friends to the same post. I requested Jefferson Barracks, outside of St. Louis. Two of my classmates had reported there and had written glowing reports of their experiences. I watched for the mail each day with a mixture of dread and anticipation.

A letter arrived about the first of March and I knew this was the "orders." I trembled as I opened the envelope. The letter read, "You are commissioned a Second Lieutenant in the United States Army. Report to Camp Chaffee, Fort Smith, Arkansas, on March 17, 1942." I threw the letter on the table. I covered my face as tears streamed out. I sobbed, "That is a hell of a birthday present!" The date was my twenty-third birthday. I'd never heard of Camp Chaffee and could find no one else who had heard of it either.

The days following the orders and my report to camp passed quickly. Along with the orders came instructions as to what we could and could not bring to camp. I realized that, until the war was over, my life was not my own. I belonged to the army now.

Until the army issued uniforms, we would wear civilian dress except on special occasions. My oldest sister sewed a blue jersey formal, trimmed with gold braid, to wear to the Saturday night dances at the officer's club. I bought an army footlocker and packed the formal, along with everything else I owned, for the trip to Camp Chaffee.

The day arrived for me to leave. Mother and Dad took me to the station in Iowa Falls to meet a train for Kansas City. I changed trains there for one that traveled to Fort Smith.

"I hope and pray this war will be over soon. I don't want you to leave the United States," said Mother anxiously.

"Oh, don't worry. I'll tell the army that I want to work here," I assured her.

"Please write soon. You know I can't write until I know your address," said Mother. She was on the verge of tears.

"It looks like your train has a diesel engine rather than steam," said Dad when the train came into view. "You'd better go because those trains move out fast and they won't wait for you."

I gave Mother a quick kiss and Dad a brief handshake. I ran toward the train and did not look back. I was already homesick and I did not want them to see me cry.

I found a seat and sat motionless until Iowa Falls was far behind me. A mixture of loneliness and exciting and apprehensive thoughts crowded my mind. How would I handle the days ahead?

A porter came into the car and his announcement jolted to me to reality.

"First call for dinner," he repeated as he made his way through the car.

I walked through several cars crowded with young men. I thought, *They too are going to a military installation somewhere.* I searched for a familiar face and did not see any.

The porter seated me at a table with a couple in their forties. They were returning home to Kansas City after visiting family in Minneapolis.

Trying to look sophisticated, I said, "I'll have a Manhattan and the steak, medium, well done." The thought that the army would pay for it also crossed my mind.

"I would also like a package of Camel cigarettes," I said, although I did not smoke.

I arrived in Kansas City about 1900 hours. I followed the crowd to the cavernous waiting room. Soldiers, sailors, nuns in their rustling habits, and civilians filled every bench. Two signs hung overhead—"White Waiting Room" and "Colored Waiting Room." I passed fountains that said "Whites Only" on my way to the "White" waiting room.

I tried to absorb all the sights. A woman with a familiar gait ahead of me caught my attention. I realized it was Margaret Finley, who finished nurse's training a year ahead of me at Iowa Methodist Hospital.

"Margaret! Margaret!" I shouted.

Margaret stopped, turned slowly, and scanned the crowd before she saw me.

"Avis! What are you doing here?"

"I'm on my way to Camp Chaffee at Fort Smith, Arkansas," I said. "Where are you going?"

"That's where I'm going!" said Margaret.

We dropped everything we were carrying and hugged. Two happy people searched, arm in arm, for the Pullman car that would take us to Fort Smith.

"Margaret, will you wake me in the morning? I don't want to oversleep."

"Of course. I brought an alarm clock."

I climbed the ladder to my upper bunk and undressed behind the heavy curtains. The rocking of the train and the secure feeling of a friend nearby formed a warm lullaby.

I soon heard a tapping on the curtain.

"Avis, are you awake? It's time to get up. The train is due in Fort Smith in one hour."

We arrived in Fort Smith at 0800 on March 17, 1942.

Chapter II

Civilian to Military

A young corporal met us at the station. This was our first meeting with someone in military uniform. We went outside to warm temperatures and bright sunshine. The change in climate refreshed us after the stuffy and confined quarters of the train. An open-sided army vehicle waited at the curb. Camp Chaffee was twelve miles south of Fort Smith.

The warm breeze tousled my hair, so I searched for a comb and lipstick. I wanted to look my best when I met the chief nurse. I heard that army regulations were stricter than nurses' training, and I wanted to get started right.

We wound our way through the streets of Fort Smith. Children played on the sidewalks and adults stood nearby to visit and watch them. Outside of town, we saw dozens of women carrying heavy loads of laundry on their heads. Almost all of them had shoes but did not wear them. They trudged along the dusty road with children following in single file like mother ducks and their ducklings.

"Margaret, have you ever seen that in Iowa?" I asked.

"No, and it certainly makes me realize that customs as well as the weather are different here."

"I love the woods and hills." I thought about the flat fields at home and decided if I couldn't be there, I liked this better.

The driver slowed and turned before stopping at small booth attended by a soldier with a rifle on his shoulder. The soldier waved for us to proceed after he and the driver exchanged a few words. We started down a gravel road with a few low, wooden structures in the distance.

"Where's the camp? This surely can't be it." said Margaret.

"It must be. I don't see anything else that could be an army post," I answered, trying to hide my disappointment.

I had dreamed of arriving at a well-laid-out army camp with paved roads, brick buildings, and tree-lined boulevards. Here were dusty gravel roads and a few wooden barracks.

The corporal stopped in front of one of the buildings that looked the same as the others.

"This is the Headquarters Building. Captain Riley's office is here and you report to her."

Captain Riley was in her late thirties. Her dark eyes were as cold as her manner, and I felt intimidated at once. She did not extend any greeting.

"Where are your orders?" she asked curtly.

I searched my purse and they were not there.

"I must have put them in my suitcase." I stammered. I felt awkward and embarrassed.

"Don't you know those are important? You carry them where they are always handy. I'm not the only one who will ask to see them. Bring them here tomorrow," she said.

I decided I did not like this woman and I would be very careful not to displease her.

"There will be an orientation meeting in the mess hall at 0800 hours tomorrow. You will be there."

"You can bet I'll be there with the orders," I told Margaret. I was in camp only a few hours and the chief nurse was already watching me.

Margaret was in one barracks and I was in another a few feet away. Although a ramp connected the buildings, a tinge of loneliness swept over me. I had already encountered an intimidating and hostile atmosphere and I needed her nearby.

Steel beds, steel dressers, a lounge chair, and matching ottoman furnished each room comfortably. Unfinished walls, with supporting studs exposed, separated the rooms and offered some privacy. The building was dormitory style with a common bathroom in the middle section. The lounge area was also in the center of the building. A telephone, a couch, and a couple of chairs furnished the lounge. This room was the hub of our social activities.

I was at the meeting at 0745 hours the next morning with my orders. We received our uniforms, both for dress and duty. Two enlisted men sat behind each of the four tables in the front of the room. We approached a table when they called our names. They took information for our dog tags and gave out our duty assignments. We reported for our shots the next day. We learned that Camp Chaffee, developed to train infantry troops and tank corps, expected between seventy-five and one hundred thousand men within the next few months.

I was among a group of about fifteen reporting to the army for the first time. A half dozen transferred in from other army installations. I was grateful to those with experience who shared their knowledge. The first piece of advice—remember that we are officers and are not allowed to date enlisted men.

We admitted patients to our station hospital for reclassification and minor illnesses. We sent more serious cases to a general hospital at one of the permanent army posts.

Our white duty uniforms did not fit well and I tried to give them shape with the wide belt. The cap had gathers in back and did not flatter anyone. I thought about the trim cap I had worn at Iowa Methodist. According to popular report, Eleanor Roosevelt designed our dress uniforms. The blazer was dark navy blue, the skirt was a lighter navy blue, and the shirt was another shade of blue. Maroon braid trimmed the overseas cap, uniform, cape, and overcoat. We had black neckties and black oxfords. We received coat-style blue seersucker dresses for leisure wear. No one regretted that we did not always wear uniforms.

The hospital was a series of barracks connected with ramps and catwalks. Each building had separate offices for the nurse and ward officer, who was a doctor. We had a fully equipped kitchen and a linen room with adjoining women's lavatory. Three medical wards were ready to admit patients.

I reported for duty my third day in camp. Two enlisted men assigned to the ward helped with the duties of bringing food, cleaning, running errands, or any task I requested. I was a commissioned officer and was in charge. These men had been in the army for several months and proceeded to educate me about army language and protocol.

I filled out an endless number of reports and everything in triplicate. I assigned patients to help with cleaning and serving the food. I wondered what any of this had to do with nursing.

The ward attendants informed me that the dining room was the mess hall where the chow (food) was prepared and served. The bathroom was the latrine. Government Issue (G.I.) referred to supplies as well as personnel. An expendable item was an item easily replaced. (Most enlisted men mentally put themselves in this group.) You were "chewed out," not scolded, if you committed an infraction. If the crime was serious, you were "court martialed" and "thrown in the brig." Patients who feigned illness were "gold-bricks." You were "brown nosing" if you sought favors from someone of higher rank. Always remember R.H.I.P., which translated into "rank has its privileges." Anyone of higher rank "outranked" you and officers always out-ranked the enlisted men. Salute all officers when out of doors. I found it awkward when the enlisted men saluted me.

I was lonely and confused about army life. I read *Gone With the Wind* and tried to convince myself that the army was better than during the Civil War. Officers from the regular army were impatient and expected those just out of civilian life to adjust quickly. New nurses arrived at camp each day. Soon, someone was in every room in the barracks. My heart sank when I found Captain Riley had a room only two doors from mine.

I was beginning to adjust to my new surroundings and approached every situation cautiously. Captain Riley surprised me when I stepped into the hall on my way to the Mess Hall one morning.

"You woke me up last night. Don't you have any consideration for others? You banged around opening drawers when you came in."

"I was home reading," I protested. I felt the blood drain from my face.

"Oh, no you weren't. I heard you come in. It had better not happen again."

On my way to meet Margaret for breakfast, I thought, "Is this woman going to harass me all the time I'm in the army?"

"Captain Riley really bawled me out this morning. She has me confused with someone else," I said to Margaret.

"I wouldn't worry about it. Someone told me this morning that she's leaving. The army is discharging her. She got married secretly."

Captain Riley left a few days later. Lieutenant Beth Holden was appointed acting chief nurse. The appointment pleased me because we were friends.

Lt. Doris (Danny) Deaver

I soon developed friendships with others in the barracks. Doris Deaver, whom we nicknamed Danny, was my closest and longest friend in the army. She was a fun-loving, freckle-faced, chubby girl from South Dakota. Danny loved to dance and often asked if I would go to the Recreation Hall barracks and listen to records with her. We compared our dates and she taught me the latest dance steps. We shared many of our most grim and profound experiences as well as the happy times in the years ahead.

Mary DeLaHunt was from Saint Paul, Minnesota. Mary was always there when I needed a friend. We had some very good times in the all-too-short time that we were at Chaffee together.

The camp changed daily. We opened new wards, more nurses arrived, and our duty settled into a pattern. We worked a twelve-hour day or a twelve-hour night with a day off in two weeks if the hospital census was low.

The spring rains started in April. The military units on the post went into the field to practice warfare under combat conditions. Soldiers found devious ways to feign illness to escape the war games. We discovered, after many came in with suspicious symptoms, that they raised their body temperature several degrees by rubbing G.I. soap in their underarms. G.I. soap was strong laundry soap made with a heavy concentration of lye. They quickly returned to duty when the doctor diagnosed them as "goldbricks."

Lt. Avis Dagit and Lt. Doris Deaver
Camp Chaffee Station Hospital

Patients with colds and fever filled the wards. A few patients should not have been in the military for health reasons.

A short, overweight Irishman came in drenched with rain and having difficulty breathing. He was asthmatic and developed pneumonia. Despite the best medical care the army had to offer, his condition became critical. He died within a few days. His death was the first I saw in the army, and it was difficult to shake the grief I felt.

Saturday was inspection day at the hospital. We aligned all beds, neatly made, with blankets folded alike, along the same board in the floor. Patients helped stack linens, clean latrines until they were spotless, and remove every speck of dust from the ward. We inspected the grounds around the wards for scraps of paper and cigarette butts. Every soldier able to leave his bed took part in this exercise. I made a quick inspection and waited for the marching footsteps of Colonel Graham, Captain Howe, Sergeant Day, and the corporal on the wooden ramp.

"Here they come. Go tell the men," I instructed the ward attendant.

"Attention!" shouted the sergeant as the entourage entered the ward. Everyone stood like a statue and looked straight ahead.

Colonel Graham relieved the tension by quickly ordering, "At ease."

"It looks like you get the orchid," said Colonel Graham after the inspection. "Everything is fine. I cannot find any problems."

We relaxed for a few moments. Next week there was another inspection and we cleaned everything again.

The atmosphere throughout the camp eased after the Saturday inspections. We looked forward to the Saturday night dances at the officers' club. Even though friendships were fragile, most could look forward to dressing in a formal and going to the dance. The club was a crowded and smoke-filled barracks. There was a bar at one end and a musical combo on a stage at the other end. This left little room for dancing, so many sat in the balcony and drank. I soon learned that drinking was a favorite pastime in the army. I was glad to get out in the fresh air and walk back to the barracks at the end of the evening.

Most of us developed a special friendship with an enlisted man. My friend was a red-headed corporal from Colonel Graham's office. I looked forward to his rounds each day to pick up the ward report. My heart quickened when I heard him whistle as he came down the ramp. I was afraid an officer might see us together. His presence was like a fresh breeze in the stiff military atmosphere.

"Where can I see you tonight?" he asked.

"Do you think we should see each other? I'm afraid someone will catch us and we could get into a lot of trouble."

"Oh, you worry too much. What time can you meet me under the water tower?" he teased.

"Danny is meeting her friend at eight o'clock so we'll come together," I promised.

The water tower was about two blocks up a knoll from our barracks. There were always many nurses and enlisted men meeting there. We were never caught in our infraction of the rules.

I do not remember this soldier's name. He transferred to another camp after I had known him only a few weeks. He brought some equilibrium to my life in those early army days.

Major O'Neill, our new chief nurse, arrived in May. She was a veteran of twenty-five years in the regular army. Her sharp features and brusque manner reminded me of Captain Riley. I wondered if everyone became harsh and unfeeling in the army. Captain O'Neill impressed everyone that she strictly enforced all rules and regulations.

We were in camp only three months when Margaret came to my room.

"Avis, I have a problem." Before I could offer a comment, she went on: "I'm in love."

"Oh, Margaret, I'm happy for you. Who is he and how did you meet?"

"That's the problem," said Margaret. "He's an enlisted man and wants to get married."

"Do you plan to wait until the war is over?"

"No, he wants to get married now because he thinks his unit will be moving out soon. I'm afraid to go to Major O'Neill. The army will discharge me if I get married. I'm so in love and I want to get married before he leaves this camp."

"Major O'Neill might be understanding. She probably had a few chances to get married but didn't because of regulations." I could see Margaret had already made up her mind.

Major O'Neill gave her blessing to Margaret. She married Blackie right away. The army discharged her and she moved back to Iowa a few days later.

With her went my closest physical link to home. New friends I had made in the past few months eased my loneliness somewhat.

Mary and I started going to breakfast together after Margaret left. She did not stop for me one morning, so I went to her room. Mary was in bed.

"I'm not going on duty this morning, Avis. I have such a headache," said Mary weakly.

"You stay in bed and I'll see you later," I promised.

I was gone only a few minutes when Major O'Neill came through the barracks and noticed Mary was still in bed.

"Why aren't you up, Lieutenant DeLaHunt?" demanded Major O'Neill.

"Major, I'm so sick I can't get up."

"What if all of us stayed in bed just because we didn't feel well? Who would run the hospital?" retorted Major O'Neill. Mary was too sick to answer.

"I'll send an officer over to examine you," said Major O'Neill when she realized that Mary was gravely ill.

Two soldiers carried Mary to the hospital on a stretcher after the officer examined her. She was critically ill with pneumonia for five days. I prayed for her recovery; the death of the Irish soldier was still fresh in my mind.

Mary did recover. The army sent her home for a month to regain her strength before returning to camp.

The camp expanded rapidly and new troops arrived daily. Hard-surfaced roads replaced the gravel paths that laced the camp. The hospital became a complex of about thirty separate buildings. It had a capacity of one thousand patients at the beginning of summer. The post exchange opened, and it was the most popular place in the hospital complex. I made many trips each day to the "PX" to have a nickel Coke with friends and patients. This, along with the greasy army food, proved disastrous to my weight. I put on thirty-five pounds and tipped the scales at 160 pounds. Fortunately, all army uniforms had a boxy shape and actually fit better than when I was thinner. Summer approached and I was miserable with all the extra weight. The weather was hot and sticky and I was on night duty. My starched uniform was as wilted as I felt when I went off duty each morning. I found it impossible to escape the oppressive heat. I covered myself with a wet sheet and placed a bowl of ice in front of the fan so I could sleep. My tour of night duty lasted two weeks. Mary returned to camp about the time I went back to day duty. The door to Mary's room was ajar when I returned to the barracks. Mary sat on her bed with her back to the door. She did not see me. I rushed in and said, "It's so good to have you back, Mary. I missed you. You look wonderful."

"I'm glad to be here and I feel fine," she said. "I realized this is where I belong when I started getting better. It didn't seem like home. Most of the men I knew are in the service. Nothing is the same. And how about you? What happened while I was gone?"

"Everything changes so fast," I replied. "Troops are moving in and out each day. New nurses arrive almost daily. Thank goodness, Danny is still here and of course Major O'Neill is still chief."

"I want to tell you about Major O'Neill," said Mary. "She was so good to me while I was sick. She came by many times a day to see if there was anything she could do for me. She even brought champagne when I could take liquids, thinking it would help my strength. She is a warm and wonderful person under that gruff exterior."

"She is fair and I am glad," I agreed.

"I do have a problem, though. My brother John wants to visit me."

"That's wonderful. What's the problem with that?" I asked.

"He's an enlisted man, a sergeant."

"Surely the army could bend the rules if your family visits," I replied.

"I really don't want to take any chances. I've already been gone a month and I don't want to create any problems. What do you think I should do?"

"I think your brother should come and we will figure out something. We could go somewhere outside of camp if we had a car."

I had driven a car a few times before I had gone to the army. I had also paid fifty cents for an Iowa driver's license. I saw Mary the next morning and told her of my idea: "Why not rent a car?"

"John wouldn't want us to spend every cent we have to rent a car. I will tell him a captain, a friend of mine, loaned it to us."

We picked John up at the hotel where he was staying in Fort Smith. We drove into the Ozark Mountains between Fort Smith and Fayetteville. It was a beautiful summer evening and we headed for "Luke Smith's." It was the most popular place in northern Arkansas for military personnel who had the luxury of a car. Mary, John, and I each ordered a steak, the specialty of the house. We reveled in leaving the army with all its rules and restrictions behind for a few hours.

All went well until our return to Fort Smith. The car stalled on the main street and we could not get it started, try as we might.

"What does the captain do when this happens?" asked John.

Mary and I looked at each other with a "What do we do now?" look.

"Maybe the battery is dead," I offered.

"Why don't you call the captain and find out what to do?" urged John.

"There's a station over there. I'll have someone come start it for us," I said. I needed a solution before John saw through our plan.

The station attendant quickly got the car started. We drove John to his quarters before catching the last bus back to camp. We both sighed with relief when we were safely on the bus. I wondered if John really believed that the car belonged to a captain. Mary and I often recalled our glorious evening of respite from the rituals of army life in the months ahead.

Chapter III

Life at Chaffee

I met Mary Henehan when I went to the shower room on a steamy summer day in July. I had heard that one of the nurses had gone home for a few days because her mother had undergone serious surgery.

"Hi," I said. "I don't think we've met. Are you new in camp?"

"Not exactly," she replied. "I reported a week ago but went home because Mom had surgery."

"Oh, you must be Mary Henehan. How's your mother getting along?"

"Oh, she's doing fine and she'll be leaving the hospital in a few days. Why don't you come to my room and have a drink with me?"

Mary was a few years older than I and had experiences I had only dreamed about. She had worked in the operating room of a large Kansas City hospital for several years. I also found out that she liked to drink and concluded that this was part of her sophistication. I seriously questioned this later when we became long-time roommates.

Mary was from a close-knit Irish family. She was the only girl in a family of seven boys. She often read excerpts to me from their warm and witty letters. It was clear that Mary was the center of the family's attention.

I met Danny in the hall after a few days. She said, "Did you hear Mary went home for her mother's funeral?"

"Oh, no! She told me two nights ago her mother was getting along just fine," I answered.

"Her mother died suddenly. She had a blood clot in the lung while she was getting ready to leave the hospital. They called Mary and she left right right away."

This news left me stunned and shaken. This could happen to any of us. I thought of home and my parents.

"I'm going to ask for a leave," I said. "I've been in the army for over four months and I'm eligible for one."

"I'm not going to ask for one yet," replied Danny. "I'm going to wait until around Christmas."

"I'll ask for one now and by the holidays I'll be ready for another one."

"Good luck," replied Danny, "but Major O'Neill won't approve it."

I couldn't put the idea of a leave out of my mind. On my next trip to the PX, I shopped for a suitcase. I didn't own any luggage except an army footlocker.

The next morning I heard the cadence of Major O'Neill's footsteps coming down the hall. My door was slightly ajar. She stopped, opened the door, and came in.

She picked up the suitcase and said, "Where did you get this?"

"I got it at the PX," I stammered.

"This is a lead-lined suitcase. Who do you think is going to carry it for you? Remember, you're in the army now and have to take care of yourself. You'll have to carry your own luggage. No one will do it for you." I felt like a six-year-old being scolded by the teacher.

I avoided others on my way to the mess hall. I needed to sort things out in my mind. I concluded I would forget about asking for a leave for a little while.

I met Danny in the mess hall.

"I have a day off tomorrow. How about you?" I asked.

"I have tomorrow off too. Let's go to Fort Smith and shop."

"Great! I've been wanting to look for a formal. I've worn the same dress every Saturday night. I want something new," I told her.

"Do you think that's a good idea?" asked Danny. "The fighting is getting worse every day. I heard some of us will go overseas soon. We'll soon have to wear a uniform all the time."

"I'll take my chances. I'll see you tomorrow at the nine o'clock bus. I have to run now."

Danny and I had a wonderful time browsing through all the stores. I found the perfect formal with a black-and-white plaid taffeta skirt and a black velvet bodice with a sweetheart neckline.

We returned to camp on the late afternoon bus, satisfied that we'd had a successful shopping trip.

We passed a parade ground where soldiers were doing marching drills.

"Let's stop and watch those soldiers," I said. "They're really good. They don't miss a step."

The drill sergeant shouted, "Halt!" and the men stopped in their tracks. We watched as the sergeant walked straight toward us.

"Don't you salute the colors when they pass? I've never seen such a breach of military discipline. I should report you to the post adjutant."

Danny and I both blanched. He returned to his troops before we could offer an excuse or apology.

"He was really mad," I said. "We may be in big trouble. I didn't notice the flag. I was watching the footwork of those men."

"We'll probably be on the next list of transfers to another post," said Danny. "Worse yet, they might send us to the federal prison at Fort Leavenworth." She laughed, making light of the reprimand.

The scolding discouraged me. I tried to follow the rules but someone always watched for a misstep. Several days passed before we concluded that the sergeant had not carried out his threat. We heard nothing more of the incident.

A week later Mary returned to camp and I often went to her room. She wanted to talk about her mother and it helped her deal with her deep grief and loneliness.

"I'm going to ask for overseas duty. We're not accomplishing anything here and I want to get this war finished," said Mary.

"I know. None of the men on my ward are really sick. Most are hoping for reclassification and a discharge. Some are allergic to woolen uniforms and others have flat feet. Anything they can think of to get out of the army. Still, I'm not anxious to go overseas, especially to the Pacific."

The chief nurse posted a list of nurses' names on the bulletin board a few days later. Those on the list were ordered to report to the parade ground for drill instruction. My name was not on the list. I concluded that I was safe from overseas duty for the time being.

There was no feeling of security even though I had escaped the drill instruction. The atmosphere throughout the camp was restless and changing. New nurses arrived so often that I no longer tried to become acquainted. Transfers to other army posts came without warning. Old friends from my earliest army days were among them. Everyone was powerless to change military orders and the transfers often brought a flood of tears before resignation and acceptance. Infantry troops and tank corps went to staging areas in preparation for overseas duty almost daily. Most went to the East Coast before going to England.

Learning close-order drill at Camp Chaffee

In early August, I decided that the time was right to request a leave. I tried to prepare myself for a lecture from Major O'Neill. She fulfilled my expectations.

Major O'Neill was sitting behind her desk when I timidly approached her.

"What do you want, Lieutenant Dagit?" she demanded without looking up.

I managed to utter, "I would like to request a leave."

"Don't you realize that we're at war and you can't have a leave anytime you want one? Why do you want it?"

"I'd like to go home and visit my family," I replied timidly.

"It would be a fine thing if everyone wanted to go home. Who do you think would staff the hospital? When do you want it?"

"I'd like the last two weeks in August if possible," I answered dejectedly.

A few days later I saw Major O'Neill in the mess hall. She stopped me and said, "You can come to my office and pick up your orders. Your leave is granted for the last two weeks in August."

I ran back to the barracks and the first person I met was Danny.

"I got it! I got my leave. Now I'll have to figure out how to get home."

I studied the train schedules and looked into the possibility of flying. Fort Smith did not have an airport but there was one in Tulsa, Oklahoma, 120 miles away. This fact along with the thirty-five dollar fare, half a month's salary, made the idea flying quite impossible.

I had a dental appointment a few days after I got my orders.

"I hope my dental work can be finished quickly," I said. "I have a leave coming up in ten days."

"That shouldn't be a problem," the dentist said. "Where are you going?"

"I'm going to Iowa if I can figure out how to get there."

"Why don't you fly?" he said. "I'm going to Philadelphia that day and you may ride to Tulsa with me. I'd enjoy having your company."

"Oh, that's great!" I said, unable to believe my good fortune.

I ran to the barracks to make my reservation.

I was busy the next ten days preparing for my trip along with twelve hours of duty each day. I would fly from Tulsa to Des Moines, the nearest airport to home.

The trip to Tulsa was pleasant despite the red, dust-choked roads. I felt a spine-tingling chill of excitement when I climbed the stairs to the waiting plane. This was my first plane ride.

The aircraft was a two-engine propeller plane that carried about twenty passengers. We traveled at a dizzying speed compared to the long train ride in March. We flew through an electrical storm and I watched the lightning curl around the wings of the plane. I was sorry the flight was over so quickly.

I took a taxi from the airport to the Rock Island train station. I waited impatiently for the train to pull out of the station for Iowa Falls, seventy miles away. I started my journey at nine in the morning. It was dark and after 9:00 P.M. when I saw Mother and my brother, Arnold, standing on the platform waiting for me.

I ran to Mother. We kissed and embraced while Arnold stood awkwardly in the background.

"It's good to be home. And how is everyone?" I asked excitedly.

"We're all fine," Mother said, "but Grandpa Arnold's knees are bothering him. Grandpa and Grandma Dagit both have heart problems. So many young people in the area have gone to war and that worries me more. This war is growing worse each day." I read the worry in her face as she spoke.

"Have they started any rationing yet?" I asked.

"No," replied Mother, "but they're talking about it. Don't worry; we're not suffering for anything."

The next two weeks passed quickly and I enjoyed the pampering, good food, restful sleep, and security of family around me. When it was time to return to camp, I was anxious to go. I realized that was where I belonged until the war was over.

I looked for Danny as soon as I returned to camp.

"Oh, I'm glad you're still here. Tell me all the news. What happened while I was gone?"

"Well, troops are still moving in and out," she said. "Several nurses were transferred but none from this barracks. There won't be any more leaves until the war is over. That's probably the biggest news.

"Oh, I almost forgot. We have a new chief of medicine. His name is Major Day and he's been in the army for thirty-five years."

"I'll probably see him tomorrow because I'm going to work days for a couple of weeks," I replied. "I wonder why they transferred an officer that age to a new camp."

When I went to work the next day I found that the army had hired a civilian to help with ward duties. The man on my ward was about fifty years old. He had a ruddy complexion and light red hair. He was toothless and had a heavy southern accent. The soldiers loved him and called him "Pop." He was full of tales about hunting and how many quail were in the fields around camp.

"I'm going hunting this weekend," said Pop. "I'll bring enough quail for everyone to have a quail dinner Monday."

I secretly hoped his hunting luck would fail. I was afraid of the consequences if the officer of the day found us cooking on the ward. Pop arrived, as promised, with enough quail for thirty, ingredients for dressing, cranberries, and mashed potatoes. Everyone put all thoughts of discipline and army chow behind them for a few hours and enjoyed the delicious meal.

The corridor outside the ward filled with the aroma of roasting quail. The officer of the day did not find out about the party—or chose to ignore it.

I was on night duty again a few days later. None of the patients were acutely ill and they slept soundly all night. I wrote letters and struggled to stay awake. I expected the night supervisor to pick up the report soon and then I could go off duty.

I had my report ready and handed it to Lieutenant Holden.

"Would you mind taking all the reports to Major Day's office for me?" Lieutenant Holden said. "You'll be going past there on your way to the barracks. It'll save me a trip."

"Of course not," I replied. "I'll be glad to do it."

I wrapped my cape around me and walked down the ramp thinking only of how good it would feel to fall into bed.

The door to Major Day's office was open, so I walked in and laid the reports on his desk. I didn't see Major Day behind the open door. Before I could turn and leave, he grabbed me and slammed the door shut. He shoved me into a corner and tried to kiss me and had his hands all over me.

"Stop it! Let me go! Let me go!" I shouted while I struggled to free myself.

I got to the door and opened it. I ran down the ramp and didn't stop running until I reached my room.

I heard a knock on my door.

"Are you all right, Avis? May I come in?" asked Mary DeLaHunt.

I went to the door because I wanted to talk to someone and I knew I could trust Mary.

"What's the matter?" said Mary. "You look like you've seen a ghost."

"Major Day attacked me," I said through my tears as I told of what happened.

"You have to tell Major O'Neill," said Mary. "How could an officer in his position do such a thing?"

"Oh, no!" I protested. "I can't say anything. He'd deny it and who'd believe me? He's a major and I'm a second lieutenant. I'd be transferred to another post."

"You're probably right," agreed Mary.

"I'm not hurt. I got away before he could do anything, but I'm angry. He's an old man," I sobbed. " He's older than my father!"

I'm glad you told me," said Mary. "I'll stay out of his way when I'm alone. Try to get some sleep now. I'll see you when you wake up."

Neither Mary nor I told anyone of the incident that had shaken our personal security. We learned to fear and respect high ranking officers in the few short months we were in the army.

The news that Americans had entered combat in North Africa reached us around the first of November. We speculated that all of us would be leaving Chaffee soon because we were fighting the Germans and Italians in addition to the Japanese. The United States suffered heavy casualties and all branches of the service needed nurses.

In the middle of November, we received orders to wear uniforms at all times and send all civilian clothes home. This was my last link with civilian life. I went to my room to pack. I closed the door and put on my beautiful brown suede pumps and yellow jersey blouse for the last time. I exchanged the colorful clothing I had bought in the past year for black, flat oxfords and navy blue uniforms.

Thanksgiving came and the meal was the only change from any other day in camp. We had turkey and all the trimmings, including large bowls of mixed nuts and fruit on each table.

"It looks like they're fattening us for the kill," was a comment heard often around the table.

The United States was getting deeper into the war each day. It was hard to think of anything else. We heard of Japanese atrocities against our men that were in Bataan and Corregidor. I prayed my next assignment would not be in the Pacific.

Christmas was coming but there was little celebrating. I went to Fort Smith to buy a few Christmas gifts, among them an expensive compact and White Shoulders perfume for Mother. I knew she couldn't afford these luxuries while we were growing up. I wouldn't have a chance to shop if I went to a little island in the Pacific, I reasoned.

The post chapel was a wooden barracks like other buildings in camp. It served as a synagogue on Saturday for the Jewish services, a church early Sunday morning for the Catholics, and a church for Protestant services at eleven. Everyone had time to attend services of their choice each week. Danny and I went to church on Christmas morning and sang the carols with more feeling than I had ever known.

Our Christmas dinner was more sumptuous than at Thanksgiving. The menu included big bowls of candy in addition to the usual turkey feast. Cocktails with our meal were offered from a bar set up in the mess hall. The noise level made it difficult to talk even with those beside you. Everyone tried to savor only the moment.

I returned to the barracks and wrote letters. My folks didn't have a tele-phone so I couldn't call home. I went to bed thinking, *I lived through one more Christmas. Where will I be on the next one?*

It was cold in Arkansas in January and snow covered the ground. The barracks were drafty and poorly heated.

The hospital wards were full of patients with fever, aches, and chills. Troops trained in the field for combat. Many of the patients were recruits not conditioned for the rigors of army life.

I was getting ready to go on duty when I heard a knock. It surprised me to see Lieutenant Holden when I opened the door.

"I'm going to have you be special nurse tonight for a very sick patient," she said. "He has pneumonia and will probably die before morning."

"What am I supposed to do?" I asked, not expecting an answer, only some assurance I could fulfill this assignment.

"Do the best you can and I'll check with you during the night," she said. "Just in case I don't get there first, you can go to Ward 33 after he expires."

I felt weak and filled with self doubts. I had not taken care of anyone who was critically ill since I was in the army. I tried to recall all I had learned about the care of pneumonia patients. I remembered the words of my nurs-ing instructor: "Nursing care is the most important treatment we have. Good care can mean life and poor care might mean death to a pneumonia patient."

I went on duty feeling a heavy burden on my shoulders. I made a silent vow to carry out this assignment with exceptional nursing care.

Private Jim Collins was in a private room. The hospital had very few of these rooms reserved for critically ill patients.

I approached his bed and felt it shake with every labored breath. The heavy growth of beard made him appear much older than his thirty-nine years. His mouth was hanging open and only white showed from his half open eyes. I felt his forehead; it was hot and dry.

"Jim," I whispered. "Are you awake?"

He did not respond.

I asked again, "Jim, are you awake?"

He was in a coma and it was a challenge to give the fluids that he desperately needed. I filled a drinking straw with water and dropped it on his parched tongue. His temperature was 104 degrees. I bathed his body with tepid water to reduce the fever. I struggled at turning him every hour. The bed was high and he weighed 180 pounds. After I finished my routine of fluids, bathing, and turning, I started over. I went off duty exhausted but relieved that my patient did not appear any worse and was still alive.

Lieutenant Holden reported the next evening that the soldier's condition appeared unchanged and I would again be his special nurse.

Jim was still in a coma and did not respond when I spoke to him. I carried out the routine I had set up the previous night.

I took his temperature at midnight and it was down to one hundred degrees. His breathing became quiet and regular and his skin was warm and moist. He slept soundly for the first time.

I was dropping water into his mouth when he opened his eyes. He said, "What day is this?"

My heart leaped with joy because I knew his fever had broken and he was recovering. I took his temperature and it was ninety-nine degrees.

I was eager to go on duty the next night and see if Jim was better. He responded weakly when I spoke to him.

"How would you like for me to shave you?" I asked.

"I suppose it would be all right," he answered with little enthusiasm. "I know I need it."

I moved from one side of the bed to the other to reach him. I spent an hour shaving him and it was bedtime when I finished.

"I think I'll sleep all night," said Jim. "I didn't know a shave could make such a difference."

He had a quiet night and I saw improvement in his condition every hour.

"I'm going to have you stay on duty with Private Collins for a couple more nights," Lieutenant Holden said. "He's making a good recovery and we want to be sure his condition continues to improve."

I looked forward to going on duty because Jim now greeted me warmly. "It's good to see you. Did you get some sleep?" he asked. "I'll miss you after tonight but I know the army won't pamper me any longer."

I received a gift of a carton of cigarettes and a note a few days after I was no longer caring for Jim. The note read, "Thanks for the wonderful care. You saved my life." He signed the card, "A grateful patient, Private Jim Collins."

Many of the nurses became restless at Chaffee. The fighting raged in North Africa and the Germans devastated London with V-2 bombs. We saw little progress in the Pacific war despite a brief air raid over Tokyo.

"Why are we still here? Why aren't we where we're needed? Let's get this war over," were comments heard everywhere.

We did not have to wait much longer.

I was sitting at my desk filling out requisition slips when Danny burst in from the adjoining ward.

"I just overheard Major O'Neill tell Lieutenant Holden that orders arrived in her office for ten nurses," said Danny excitedly. "Do you suppose we're on the list? We've been here longer than anyone else."

I thought I was mentally prepared for anything but the news left me numb and confused.

"If my friends receive orders, I hope I'm included. We'll find out soon enough," I finally managed to say.

I saw Lieutenant Holden at lunch.

"Danny said orders came for ten nurses. Can you tell me if I'm one of them?" I asked.

"I wish I could, but I can't say anything before Major O'Neill tells everyone," she said. "It's a very exciting assignment and I'd love to be on that list myself."

I went back to the ward unable to concentrate on anything. What would the next few hours hold for me? One of the new nurses came to the ward in the late afternoon.

"I'm here to relieve you so you can report to Major O'Neill's office," she said.

I was both excited and frightened as I walked quickly to Major O'Neill's office. I was glad I didn't meet anyone because my throat was so tight I couldn't speak.

When I walked into Major O'Neill's office, she stood and handed me two typewritten sheets of paper.

"These orders came through for you today, Lieutenant Dagit," she said. "This a hazardous assignment and you will be working under combat conditions. You'd better think about sending everything home except the bare essentials. There'll be ten of you leaving together."

The orders read, "You will report to Fort Sam Houston, Texas, on February 18, 1943, where you will join the 56th Evacuation Hospital. The hospital is in the Staging Area awaiting assignment for overseas duty."

I saw a troubled look on Major O'Neill's face that I had not seen before. I quickly left her office and ran to the barracks to find out who else was going to Fort Sam.

I heard the noise before I reached the door and knew the party had started.

"Come in, Dagit!" shouted Mary as she put a drink in my hand. "You'd better start packing."

"We're on our way. We'll soon get this war over," chimed in another.

Among the celebrants were Danny, Mary, and two other nurses with whom I would share many moments in the years ahead: Ellen and Lena.

Lena was from southern Minnesota, a full-blooded German and proud of it. She was six feet tall and her character was equal to her physical strength.

Ellen Ainsworth was a free spirit from Wisconsin. We would soon know "On Wisconsin" better than our own state song. Ellen loved to sing and started a song fest at every opportunity. Ellen was

Lt. Ellen Ainsworth

especially eager for overseas duty. She was friendly and outgoing and liked to shock those around her. I remembered seeing her at the Saturday dance at the officers' club. She was dancing, holding a pint of whiskey (from which she took several nips), and smoking a cigar. Ellen was born when her only brother and sister were teenagers. She loved her independence. We soon became good friends.

"We're are supposed to pack all the personal supplies we'll need for a year," said Mary.

"How can we tell how much soap, shampoo, and toothpaste we'll need?" asked Danny.

"And how about Kotex?" asked another.

"What are we supposed to tell our families? Will we be able to tell them we're going overseas?" I asked.

I felt out of touch with myself. My head ached and my stomach was in knots. Why did I have this feeling of foreboding when everyone else was celebrating? Major O'Neill's warning was still ringing in my ears. I thought about home and the promises I'd made to my parents. The realization that one did not have a choice in the army rocked my emotions.

We left the party with more questions than answers. Our tour of duty at Chaffee ended abruptly. We packed all unnecessary clothing and personal items and mailed them home in the next two days.

I was sorry Mary DeLaHunt was not among the ten. Those from Chaffee became a cohesive group in the years ahead despite our diverse personalities.

Chapter IV

Charting the Unknown

I spent the next two days writing letters and visiting with a few friends whom I was leaving at Chaffee. I made one last trip to the PX and bought two pair of nylons, which were increasingly hard to find. Rayon hose were baggy and one of the few articles of clothing the army did not regulate.

I slept fitfully my last night at Chaffee. I had visions of arriving in the thick of battle with no idea of what to do. Would the army give us a chance to tell our families we were leaving the United States? And where were we going? Why was I so confused and frightened when others thought it was an exciting assignment? I was glad when morning came and I could talk to Danny. She confessed that the same thoughts ran through her mind.

We packed and were ready to leave at 0800 on February 16. The cars did not come to take us to the station until 1000. We had an impromptu party given by Mary and Ellen while we waited. Ellen led the singing and shouting when we left the barracks.

The train was waiting on the tracks when we arrived at the station. I packed carefully and eliminated everything I could from my luggage. Despite my efforts, I struggled up the steep steps to the waiting car. I carried a coat, suitcase, purse, and hand luggage.

A station worker directed us to a car crowded with passengers, mostly young civilian women and small children.

"I wonder where they dug up this car?" said Mary.

The car had bare wooden floors. The seats were wicker and did not have padding.

"I think it's left from the last war," replied Ellen.

I looked around for an empty seat. "Where are we supposed to sit?" I asked.

"Looks like we'll have to sit on our suitcases until someone gets off," said Danny.

"I hope they aren't all going the same place we are."

Danny and I dashed for an empty seat when a couple of passengers got off. The car smelled of cigarette smoke, lunches packed by the civilians, and at least twenty babies in the car.

We opened a window for some fresh air. The train stopped at every little hamlet and belched soot each time it started. Black, oily flecks and streaks covered our faces and clothing. Our woolen uniforms became warmer as we traveled south.

"We'd better take turns going to the dining car so we won't lose this seat," said Danny. "Mary and Ellen can go first. I think Ellen needs some food to sober her up a little."

The dining car was a relief from the bedlam in the crowded passenger coach. It was much quieter when we returned to our seats after dinner. It was dark and many of the crying babies and restless toddlers were asleep.

"We are due in Ada in about an hour and that is where we'll change trains," said Mary. "We're supposed to have pullman berths tonight."

We stumbled off the train onto the dimly lit platform at 1030 hours. We saw the waiting train on the tracks about half a block away. Danny and I fell behind the rest of the group even though we hurried along the platform.

"I have too much to carry," said Danny as she paused to catch her breath. She deposited the brown paper bag that held a fifth of whiskey on a mail cart. "It'll give someone a pleasant surprise in the morning."

We often recalled this when we drank cocktails of canned grapefruit juice and medical alcohol in the years ahead.

The long, tedious ride from Fort Smith was exhausting. We welcomed the luxury of freshly made berths when we got on the train. Mary and I agreed to share a compartment.

"I never get up at night, so I'll take the top bunk," I volunteered. Mary still felt the effects of her drinking.

I fell asleep quickly and slept soundly. Bright sunshine came through a crack in the curtain when I woke up.

The landscape in Texas was as flat and monotonous as Oklahoma. We saw the cars ahead of us, crowded with military personnel, when the train rounded a curve. People of all ages filled the platform at every small town. Their eyes searched for familiar faces on the troop train. They made the V for victory sign, shouted their encouragement, and cheered when the train pulled slowly out of the station.

"Did anyone bring a deck of cards?" asked Ellen.

"I did," said Mary. "What game shall we play?"

"Let's play pinochle," I said. "We'll need another deck of cards." I began to search my hand luggage.

"I found one," exclaimed Danny.

"Let's make it more interesting by playing for five cents on the hand and twenty-five cents on the game," said Mary.

"That sounds good. No one will lose much money," agreed Ellen.

We played pinochle all day, stopping only long enough to go for meals. We soon forgot about the hard mohair seats and the dull landscape dotted with pumping oil wells.

The train arrived in San Antonio in the early evening. A military bus waited to take us to Fort Sam Houston, a short drive outside of town.

"I'd love to take off this jacket," I said to Danny. "I hope we get something cooler for summer wear." It was hot and the trees were fully leafed out. We were in the deep south.

We rode down paved, tree-shaded boulevards toward our quarters. "Fort Sam" was an old army post. All the buildings were red brick and the largest, Brooke General Hospital, dominated the skyline. The carefully attended grounds were immaculate, and every blade of grass stood at attention.

"The bulletin board in the lounge of your quarters will carry all the information you'll need," said the captain who met us. "There'll be an orientation meeting in the recreation hall tomorrow and the bus will pick you up at 0900 hours."

Our rooms were lavishly furnished with warm, wooden beds; dressers; rugs; and easy chairs. The regular peace-time nurses lived well. The rooms were a treat after the cold, drafty barracks at Chaffee. I did not waste time getting undressed; I headed for the hot showers a few steps down the hall. Sleep came quickly after two hard days of travel.

Spirits were high while we waited for the bus to take us to the meeting. The officers and nurses with the 56th Evacuation Hospital, which was activated on March 29, 1942, were already in the hall. They filled the first two rows of chairs. Everyone turned and looked when we entered. Danny and I quietly seated ourselves in the back of the room.

"They're really looking us over," I whispered to Danny.

"I heard they've been on maneuvers in Louisiana," said Danny. "We probably look pretty green to them."

Doctors and nurses from Baylor Medical School in Dallas, Texas, formed the early organization. Ten nurses from a camp in Louisiana were also joining the hospital staff. The personnel of the hospital now consisted of 48 officers, 49 nurses, and 315 enlisted men. The 56th Evacuation Hospital was a 750-bed facility equipped to handle patients under field conditions.

Colonel Blesse, the commanding officer, had many years of service in the regular army. He was easily approachable, but he did demand strict obedience to army regulations and protocol. His reputation for drinking soon became legendary throughout the organization.

"Attention!" called a sergeant when Colonel Blesse entered the meeting.

"We are on twenty-four-hour alert," he began. "No more leaves are granted, and we have to be ready to go at any time. Wear your dog tags. From now on, refer to this organization only by the shipping number, which is 5920G. Any questions?"

I felt my chest tighten and looked for some reaction from others.

"Where will we be going?" asked someone.

"Can we tell our family?" asked another.

"How will we travel?"

Colonel Blesse offered no answers to any of the questions. We were sure we would be leaving Fort Sam in a few days, but it was six weeks before we received orders to report to the port of embarkation.

We filled our days with meetings and trips to San Antonio. The time passed quickly. Someone decided the nurses should learn close-order drill. It was hot, and gale-force winds made each day seem hotter.

"It's going to be hot out there in the sun," said Mary. "I'm going to take something to drink."

"I am, too," agreed Ellen. "What are you taking?"

"I'm filling my canteen with Coke," said Mary.

We discovered later that Mary and Ellen had added a generous amount of whiskey to their canteens.

The longer we marched, the more the ranks became ragged. I sensed the frustration of the drill sergeant. After a few futile attempts to make us into foot soldiers, the program was abandoned.

We added equipment for use in a combat area to our ever-increasing pile of luggage. Along with helmets, mess kits, musette bag, coveralls, and gas masks was gas-proof clothing. The heavy denim trousers and tops were treated with material to make them gas proof. Aside from being stiff and having a metallic odor, the fact that we might ever need to wear them had a chilling effect on me.

We had many meetings to practice donning the gas masks and gas-proof clothing. The day arrived when we found out whether we had learned our lesson well. We put on our equipment according to military regulations, which the army called "by the numbers." The blazing sun bore down on us while we waited for our turn to enter the chambers. Two soldiers stood at each end of the chamber, which was a few feet below ground. We entered one at a time.

"There's nothing to it," said the first nurse when she came out of the chamber.

The next in line came out screaming and crying hysterically. She had gotten a good dose of the tear gas that filled the chamber.

I checked my mask again. The corporal called my number. I ran through the chamber as fast as I could while holding my breath. I flung off the mask when I reached daylight and took a deep breath. I passed the test.

There was a meeting for us to make a will, appoint power of attorney, and fill out insurance and allotment forms. The experience sobered me because I realized even more that we had a dangerous assignment. I took a seat at a table that served as a desk. The handsome blond soldier greeted me warmly, and that relieved the tension somewhat. I was ignorant in legal

River walk in San Antonio

matters and he was kind and helpful. I did not know that Jim Powers would be my most faithful and devoted friend for the rest of my army days.

We took advantage of our time at Fort Sam and got away from camp at every opportunity. We were on twenty-four-hour alert and did not venture far.

"How'd you like to go to San Antonio tomorrow?" I asked Danny.

"I'd love it! This sitting around waiting is getting to me."

"Let's take the nine-o'clock bus and then we can come home early," I said.

We went through every department store but dared not buy anything.

"Let's go for a walk along the river," said Danny. "After that, it should be time for lunch. We don't want to go back to camp yet."

We seated ourselves in the shade along the river and waited for time to pass. Two soldiers from the air force came and sat on the bench near us.

"Hi," said one.

"Where are you from?" asked the other.

"Fort Sam," answered Danny. "Where're you from?"

"Kelly Field," one answered.

"What state are you from?" was the next question I asked.

"We're both from Iowa, just outside of Des Moines."

"I'm from Iowa too!" I exclaimed. I felt an immediate friendship with the two airmen.

"What are your plans for the rest of the day?" one asked.

"We really don't have any," I confessed.

"How about having dinner with us at the St. Anthony Hotel?" asked the other man.

"We'll meet you here at six o'clock," they said, and they sauntered off.

We met promptly at six and walked a few blocks to the hotel. We crossed a spacious lobby filled with overstuffed chairs and a milling crowd of civilians and military personnel. Several large crystal chandeliers, hung from a two-story ceiling, cast a dim light in the dining room. Small tables, covered with white linen cloths, crowded around a tiny dance floor. The headwaiter escorted us to a table on the edge of the floor.

A big band played the latest tunes. A lump came to my throat when they played "Sentimental Journey." The evening passed quickly as we laughed and talked. I glanced at my watch.

"Danny, we'd better go! The last bus leaves in ten minutes."

We said a hasty "good-bye and good luck" and hurried out of the dining room.

We ran two blocks to the bus and got there just as the driver was preparing to close the door.

We sat down and caught our breath. I said to Danny, "Those fellows were real gentlemen, but I can't even remember their names."

"Neither can I," she confessed. We made friendships in a hurry and they were fleeting. There were no strangers in uniform; everyone was a friend.

There was an officers' call on February 19. We instinctively knew that the orders we had been waiting for had arrived. We gathered in the mess hall at Brooke Hospital, where Colonel Blesse made the announcement.

"Our orders came," he began. "All equipment will be ready by February 27 and personnel by March 13."

There were no shouts of joy. I thought of home and where I would spend my birthday. I recalled the past year and wondered what my next year in the army would bring.

We were afraid to venture outside camp because we knew the orders to move might come at any time. We received instructions in the procedure to follow at the train station. The day arrived for our departure. We left the San Antonio station promptly at 1300 hours on March 31, 1943.

Chapter V

Off to War

The nurses were on one pullman car and the officers on another. The enlisted men and our equipment made up the rest of the train.

Some of the personnel had fortified themselves with liquor and others sat quietly, almost unnoticed, amid the bedlam and shouting. Were we on our way to the West Coast or New York? We soon passed through small towns in East Texas and concluded that we were on our way to New York.

It was springlike in Texas. The farther east and north we went, the more we realized it was still winter. The trip took four days and much of that time the sky was gray and overcast. The trees were still barren of leaves, and to add to the bleakness of the landscape, we passed through a blizzard in Ohio. One day melded into another on the trip. We moved out of the flat plains of Texas to the farmlands of Ohio. We entered the low mountains and hills of Pennsylvania and New York on the third day of the trip.

Our two meals a day were adequate because playing cards was our only exercise. The pullman berths did afford us a good night's sleep.

"I've played enough pinochle today," said Ellen. "There's a poker game in the next car. Should we join the fellows?"

"Not me," I said. "I don't know how to play poker and those fellows would wipe me out in a minute."

"I'll be back in time for dinner," said Ellen when she left.

Ellen returned after she had been gone only thirty minutes.

"How much did you win?" I asked.

"Win?" Ellen replied. "I didn't win anything. I'm broke. Those fellows are card sharks."

We dealt the cards and played more pinochle. I did not hear any more about playing poker for the remainder of the trip.

Card games were the number one activity and drinking was a close second. Supplies were running low when we reached Ohio and some brave souls decided to do something about it. When the train stopped briefly in Cincinnati, they dashed across the bridge into Kentucky to buy more liquor. We anxiously awaited their return as the train prepared to move out of the station.

We crowded the windows and shouted to the men when they came into view.

"Hurry! Hurry! We're leaving!"

They boarded the train with their purchases as the train moved slowly along the tracks.

We arrived at Camp Shanks at 2000 hours on April 3. It was mass confusion at the camp. No one knew where to find our quarters. Finally, a captain arrived and gave directions. He sent the nurses to one part of the camp and the officers and men to another. We found our sparsely furnished barracks at 2330 hours and had a good night's sleep.

Camp Shanks was new and we were the first troops in this part of the camp. Recent rains made the clay soil dangerously slippery. There were no roads or sidewalks. One of the nurses fractured her leg and many had severe sprains.

Seven thousand troops packed the mess hall at each meal. When Mary and I went to lunch the next day, we found the long lines discouraging.

"Why don't we try the post exchange?" I said. "We'll never get through this line."

Men, standing shoulder to shoulder, jostled each other for a place at the lunch counter. We pushed our way through the crowd.

"It looks like we'll have to settle for a hot dog," said Mary. They were out of everything else on the scant menu.

It was my first experience drinking from an aluminum cup. The black, oily coffee seared my lips with the first sip. I learned that the cup stayed hot much longer than the liquid it contained. Despite the experience, the hot dog on the dry roll tasted good.

There was an officer's call our second day in camp. Colonel Blesse entered the cafeteria where we had assembled. Everyone expected to hear that we would leave Camp Shanks within hours.

"We'll not leave here for a few days," he began. "I'm granting permission for you to go to New York City if you wish. Buses will leave from in front of the administration building at 1200 hours. You'll meet the bus for your return at the station a block from Times Square. The last bus is at 2200 hours."

We left the meeting eager to get started on our trip. Mary, Ellen, and I decided we would go together.

"We should write a list of places we'd like to see," said Ellen.

"Why don't we get off bus at the first subway stop? We can stop anywhere on our way to Times Square," said Mary.

Camp Shanks was in New Jersey. We crossed the Hudson River on the George Washington Bridge. We had a sweeping view of the mighty Hudson on our easy bus trip to Manhattan.

We got off the bus at the first stop on Manhattan Island and boarded the subway. The spotless cars, with few passengers, sped quietly along the route to the heart of the city. When we emerged from the underground

station, we found ourselves surrounded by skyscrapers and tried to identify them.

"That's the Flatiron Building!" I exclaimed. Lighted headlines circled
the top telling of V-2 bombs falling on London.

We were in the midst of sights we had only read about. Awestruck, we
gawked at the theaters of Broadway, the Camel Cigarette sign that blew
smoke rings, the Empire State Building, Saint Patrick's Cathedral, and Rockefeller Center.

"If we go to the top of the Empire State Building, we can get our bear-
ings from there," said Mary.

An elevator whisked us to the observation deck on the 102nd floor. We
emerged from the elevator to breathtaking views. The *Normandie* was lying
on her side at one of the docks on the East River. We had read a few weeks
before of the disastrous fire on the French luxury liner. Central Park was
an oasis of trees and grass in the middle of the bustling city. The roof of
Saint Patrick's Cathedral formed a cross below us. I paused to reflect on
what the cross would mean to me in the days ahead.

Our next stop was the cathedral. Mary knelt before the altar at St.
Patrick's and said her rosary. I said my own prayers.

"Let's go to Central Park and take a carriage ride," I said. "My aching
feet could use the rest."

"I'd still like to check out that little bar off Rockefeller Center ice rink,"
said Mary.

"Let's make our visit to the bar short so we won't miss our ride back to
camp," I reminded the others.

We sat at the window overlooking the ice rink. The young skaters looked
so carefree as they glided across the ice. I wondered if they knew the United
States was fighting a war.

We paid our bill and left, and Ellen said, "We'd better go because we'll
be in big trouble if we miss the bus."

*Lts. Mary Henehan, Ellen Ainsworth, Anne
Graves, and Doris Maxfield in New York City*

Everyone on the bus exchanged stories of their sightseeing. Realizing that we had missed a lot, we hoped for another chance to visit the city. We had permission to go to New York again a few days later.

Our first stop on the next trip was Macy's on Fifth Avenue. Ellen and Mary both spent twenty dollars on swim suits.

"Why don't you buy one, Avis?" asked Mary.

"I can't swim," I said, "and besides I only have twenty dollars left. I don't want to go overseas completely broke." I also wondered when and where we would swim during a war.

We went to dinner at the Waldorf Astoria Hotel. The maître d' seated us at a table in the middle of the dining room. A band played on stage at the end of the room. The music stopped and the master of ceremonies said,

"We have some young ladies here in uniform. Would you join me in welcoming them?"

The crowd applauded and we stood up. Women in uniform were uncommon and the diners showed their appreciation.

We went to the night club, Leon and Eddie's, after dinner. The dimly lit bar had very few patrons. We each had a cocktail.

"This place is pretty dull," said Mary. "Why don't we go to the Stork Club?"

The Stork Club was even darker and two booths each held a couple. The bartender barely looked up when we entered. We paused briefly to look around and left.

The bright lights of the Roseland Ballroom beckoned us. We found it crowded with soldiers and girls in heavy makeup trying to seduce them.

"We don't belong here," I said. "It's about time to catch the bus and I've seen enough of New York today."

I saw the highlights of New York City and found the experience exciting beyond my imagination. The walking, the sightseeing, and the rocking bus lulled me to sleep a few minutes into the trip back to camp.

"Come on, Avis," said Ellen when we reached camp. "You can sleep when you get to your room."

The next day, we packed and repacked our equipment. We wrote last-minute letters, although we could not tell what we were doing. Everyone had a rumor to relate about where we were going and when.

Official word came a few days later that we would leave Camp Shanks on April 15. We received instructions in the procedure for loading the ship. Our equipment and supplies were ready to put on the bus at 1300 hours. We wore full-dress uniform for the trip to the dock. Everyone struggled with the huge pile of equipment that we all carried. I wore my coat and belt with canteen. The gas mask, gas-proof clothing, helmet, musette bag, and purse completed the load.

We stripped our beds and waited for the bus. It did not arrive at 1300 hours as scheduled. The party started. While we waited, there was more time for drinking.

"The bus is here!" someone shouted.

I gathered my belongings once more and looked around for Mary. I went to her room and saw her lying face down on her bed. To my horror, she had fallen asleep with a cigarette in her hand. A small fire smoldered and smoke rose from the spot where the mattress had started to burn. I dashed to the bathroom and filled two glasses with water and poured it into the burning hole.

"The bus is here!" I shouted. "We have to go!"

"Go away! I'm not going!" said Mary in a belligerent tone.

"We have to," I argued. "We don't have a choice."

"Well, you go without me. I'm not going."

I ran downstairs and boarded the waiting bus.

"Where's Mary?" asked Ellen.

I looked up to see Mary slip quietly onto the bus. Shaken by the events of the last thirty minutes at Camp Shanks, I did not have time to worry about the next few hours. Ellen started singing and ignored the dark glances cast her way. Others spoke quietly, speculating on what lay ahead for us. We had averted a crisis for the moment. I kept my eyes on Mary, grateful to see her safely on the bus. The trip took us through the Holland Tunnel to a ferry waiting to take us to the dock.

The sun dropped slowly below the horizon. We crowded the deck of the ferry for our last glimpse of the Statue of Liberty. Helmeted men and women were packed shoulder to shoulder, each with their own thoughts, on the way to war.

It was 1930 hours when we filed onto the dock on Staten Island. The tall gray ship, several stories high, loomed above us in the darkness. We lined up, loaded with our gear, and waited for the captain to call our names.

"Lieutenant Avis Dagit," shouted the captain.

I answered, "N-732755." My heart pounded, and even though my legs felt like they belonged to someone else, I walked up the gangplank. I dared not stop despite the burden of loneliness, fear, and equipment I carried. Would I ever see the United States again?

Military police, shouting orders, met us at the end of the gangplank. "Don't stop! Keep moving! Stay to your right! Don't block the passageways!"

They called our names alphabetically, so Danny and I were in the same state room. We wandered through many corridors, up and down stairs, and squeezed past others before finding our quarters.

"I'm going to take this one," I said. I dropped my baggage on the first bunk inside the door.

"I'll take the one above you," said Danny. "I don't want the top one in case we have to abandon ship."

"I know we're supposed to stay in our quarters," said Danny, "but let's go see what we can find out."

We met a sailor outside our room and bombarded him with questions.

"When do we join the rest of the convoy?" I asked.

His answer was far from reassuring. "We won't be going in a convoy. We're sailing unescorted."

"Won't we even have a destroyer with us?" asked Danny. "What if we're attacked?"

"Oh, don't worry," he said with confidence. "This ship can outrun any vessel the Germans have. We're clearly marked with red crosses and we have several big guns mounted on the ship. We'll zigzag and they'll have a hard time hitting us."

"Where are we going?"

"I'm sorry, I can't answer that question," he replied. "They don't tell us."

Danny and I returned to the stateroom more apprehensive than before.

SS Mariposa, *our ship for the voyage to Casablanca*

The bunks were three deep with eighteen inches clearance between. Our beds for the days ahead were strips of bare canvas attached to steel frames with tightly stretched ropes. A neatly folded blanket was on the foot of each bunk.

"What are we going to do with all this gear?' I wondered. We could barely squeeze between the bunks in the crowded room.

"I want to keep everything handy," said Danny. "I won't feel bad if I lose that impregnated [gas-proof] clothing, but I want my helmet. I'm going to wear it to bed."

We fell into a troubled sleep thinking that we'd had our last glimpse of the United States for a while.

We awoke the next morning to find that the ship had been safely anchored in New York Harbor all night. The engines started while we were at breakfast and the ship eased slowly away from the dock. A small tug escorted us for a short distance and New York was soon out of sight.

We learned that we were aboard the *Mariposa,* a luxury liner that had formerly sailed from San Francisco to Honolulu. The ship, built for one thousand passengers, had been converted to a troop ship for five thousand. All doors, padded with pink satin, attested to the luxurious quarters in peacetime. Bathroom fixtures were made of marble. Two passengers had shared a stateroom that now held fifteen. The gleaming white ship had been painted battleship gray. Saltwater flowed from all the taps except for two hours out of twenty-four. Soap became encased in a hard shell in saltwater. We took turns and did our laundry, shampooing, and bathing in the few minutes allotted to us. Long tables replaced the round ones that had been removed from the dining room. We ate our two meals a day seated on benches. Black curtains draped all doorways, passages, and portholes to prevent a crack of light showing. We were under strict blackout conditions and no one dared light a cigarette on deck at night. Guards, posted throughout the ship, prevented anyone throwing even a cigarette butt overboard.

We always wore life jackets and kept our helmets handy. Standing under gray, overcast skies on the top deck, shortly after leaving New York Harbor, we had our first "abandon ship" drill. A soft rain mixed with spray from the ocean added to the chill atmosphere. The captain, who led the drill, pointed to the lifeboat assigned to each section. We memorized the location of the boat assigned to us in case of an emergency. I looked at the thousands on deck, the tiny boats, and the endless ocean. I concluded I would probably go down with the ship if the Germans attacked. We had drills daily and no one dismissed them as a waste of time.

We learned more about our fellow passengers when we could move about the ship. There were air force personnel along with the several medical units on board.

"There are a couple of nurses with the 95th Evac from Iowa, Avis," said Ellen.

"Who are they?" I asked.

"I don't remember their names," said Ellen, "but one of them knows you. I just saw them on the top deck."

I raced to the top deck and found Gertrude Morrow, who had graduated from Iowa Methodist the year I entered as a student. I also met Blanche Sigman, the head nurse of the 95th, from Fort Dodge, a neighboring town in Iowa.

Lt. Gertrude Morrow

"How long have you been in the service?" asked Gertrude.

"I went in right after Pearl Harbor," I answered

"I did too," said Gertrude. "I'm glad we're finally getting overseas. I didn't join the army to fill out requisition slips."

I saw Gertrude often during the next week. It reinforced the feeling that no matter what you had done in civilian life, we were now equals. We were nurses on our way to care for battle casualties.

The skies cleared on our fourth day at sea. Danny and I went to the top deck to sit in the sunshine after our routine drills. The sun on the water made each ripple glitter like diamonds as far as the eye could see. I was drowsy from the gentle rocking of the ship and the swishing sound of the wake as we moved quietly along.

"Let's go down to our room," I yawned. "The water comes on soon and we'll get to the bathroom first."

I stepped through the black curtain into what I thought was a corridor leading to a stairs to the lower deck. Instead, I walked into thin air and crashed in a heap on the landing at the bottom of the steps.

"Avis! Avis! Where are you? Are you hurt?" cried Danny.

"I hurt my leg" I managed to say after I got my breath. Warm blood filled my shoe. I saw a gaping four-inch gash exposing the bone on my right shin.

Soldiers standing nearby heard the crash and commotion. "We'd better take you to the infirmary," said one of them. With a soldier on each side, Danny and several others following, I hobbled to the infirmary.

I dropped on the first chair I saw while someone called the officer of the day.

"How did it happen?" he asked.

One of the soldiers volunteered the answer. "She'd been on deck and her eyes hadn't adjusted when she stepped on the stairs."

"Bring me a suture tray and I'll sew it up," said the captain.

I found that I hadn't suffered any hurt compared to what I went through in the next ten minutes. The doctor did not wash his hands, use sterile gloves or drapes, and gave no local anesthetic. I wanted to scream out with pain while he sewed with a big cutting needle and heavy suture. Very soon, the room began to spin. I perspired and I was nauseated.

"Give me some air!" I gasped. I flung off the life jacket.

I heard someone say, "She's going to pass out!" Another started fanning and pushed my head between my knees. My head cleared and the doctor finished the suturing.

"You're as pale as a ghost," said Danny. "We'd better get to our room."

I limped to the stateroom with a lot of help from Danny. I had a bandage from my ankle to my knee.

I didn't go to the dining room with Danny. The accident left me physically shaken. I lay on my bunk and vowed I would never allow myself to be as cold and unfeeling as the captain in the infirmary. My leg healed in about a month with only a scar to show for my war wound.

One day was much the same as another. We sat on deck and played cards by the hour. Rumors and baseless stories kept our days lively. We heard about sighting a U-boat. Another rumor had us heading back to the States because the Germans had surrendered. Someone heard that England was our destination. Fish jumping out of the water caused a lot of excitement. Others believed we were approaching land because they saw birds. All the rumors proved untrue.

We traveled during Holy Week and services were held in the lounge for all faiths. Troops packed the room at every service. We fervently prayed to God for protection.

Some of the nurses were seasick as soon as the ship left the dock. After a few days of rough water, more became sick and the dining room was less crowded. Toward the end of the trip, it was no longer necessary to eat in shifts. We changed from our fatigue coveralls into a full uniform for each trip to the dining room. I looked forward to mealtime more than any other activity.

We had been at sea six days when we got the first inkling of our destination. Everyone received two little brown books: one titled *Customs of North Africa* and the other *Language of North Africa*. We knew the fighting was going well for the Allies in North Africa and speculated that we would service the troops. We spent many hours the next few days practicing our French and Arabic phrases.

We retired early, our last night aboard ship. Everyone wanted a good night's sleep before we met the enemy. The trip had taken eight days and all looked forward to the end of our "cruise."

We had breakfast at 0500 hours and were ready to disembark at 0600. Danny and I got up at 0430 to make a last-minute check of our equipment.

"Let's go to the upper deck," I said. "Maybe we can see land."

We learned that our landing would be in Casablanca, a city in Morocco, North Africa. The sun came up and the sky was crystal clear. We sighted an irregularity on the horizon that looked like land. The outline of buildings began to take shape as we approached the harbor. Planes came out and circled the ship. Corvettes, small maneuverable escort ships, and mine sweepers guided us slowly toward shore. Silver barrage balloons, gas-filled blimps anchored with steel cables that would slice the wings off low-flying aircraft, glistened in the morning sun. Twisted steel and hulls of sunken ships testified to the fierce fighting that had occurred a few months earlier. We identified the Anfa Hotel where President Roosevelt and Prime Minister Churchill had met recently to plan war strategy. The hotel was an imposing white structure on a hill overlooking the Mediterranean. Low green hills in the background contrasted with the sandy beaches and sea. We crowded the decks to watch the ship ease into the harbor. I paused to offer my personal thanks to God that we had made the trip safely and would soon be on terra firma. A small band was on the dock playing the latest American tunes to welcome us.

"How's everything in the States?" shouted a soldier on the dock.

"Where're you from?" asked another.

"Did you bring any comic books or magazines?" was another question. Some shouted, "Sucker! You'll be sorry!"

"How long have you been here?" shouted someone from the ship.

"Five months and I'm sick of the place. I'm ready to go home," was the reply.

We received our debarkation plan. Unit after unit left the ship and our turn did not come. Lunchtime came, so we ate the precious C rations we had saved for an emergency. The band had left long ago. We went ashore at 1500 hours on April 24, 1943.

Chapter VI

Morocco

Men in white baggy pants and red fezzes crowded around the dock. Their dress showed they were Moslems. Adults pushed children, many grotesquely deformed and crippled, to the front. They begged for smokes, chocolate, gum, or anything else we threw to them. They had learned quickly from the Americans who had arrived before us. Dark-skinned little urchins held two fingers high in a V for victory. A choking odor of garbage and rotting fish along with human and animal waste hung over the entire area.

The nurses boarded the back of a two-and-a-half-ton truck for the trip to our quarters. The men and officers marched to their camp three miles from the dock.

We stared at the Arabs as we rode through town and they stared at us. Walls, topped with jagged glass, surrounded the white buildings with red-tile roofs. The stucco walls were ablaze with brilliant red and purple bougainvillaea in the hot cloudless sky. Veiled women, swathed in shapeless muslin garments, prodded donkeys along the the palm-lined boulevards. Most had babies on their backs and balanced loads of wood, bags of grain, or jugs of water on their heads. Men rode on donkeys a short distance behind them. Donkeys, camels, dogs, and horse-drawn carriages were everywhere. Charcoal-burning buses loaded with people, chickens, and rabbits chugged along the streets. Those that couldn't get inside rode on top of the vehicle. The smell of filth filled the air.

Place de la France, the square in the center of town, held a sign erected by the Americans. It told the mileage to New York, London, Rome, Berlin, and Tokyo.

"We're a long ways from home," I said to Danny. "It'll be a long time before we see New York again. I wonder how the war is going."

"I'd like to hear some news,'" she said. "Maybe we can find a *Stars and Stripes* somewhere. I sure can't read Arabic or French."

The truck stopped in front of École Internat Premier, a French primary school. Our quarters were on the second floor. The long room was divided into cubicles with half walls separating them. A small table and a cot with steel springs and a lumpy mattress furnished each cubicle.

When Mary sat on the bed, she said, "This sure isn't a Beautyrest. We won't be here long, so I can stand it."

"Have you been to the bathroom yet?" said Ellen. "I've never seen one like it."

The floor of the toilet had two steel plates where you planted your feet. There was a six-inch hole between the plates. Water swirled over the entire floor when we pulled the chain on the overhead tank. We stepped lively to avoid wet feet when we flushed the toilet. The shower was in the basement.

"We're supposed to take our impregnated clothing downstairs," said Ellen. "They're coming to collect it."

"That was a pretty clever way for the army to get that heavy stuff over here," I replied dryly. "I'm glad to get rid of it."

Arab children in Casablanca

The officers' and nurses' mess hall was on the ground floor of our building. Sgt. Milonowitz and Sgt. Blackie from Brooklyn and Cpl. Carl Moon from Lexington, Kentucky, were our cooks. We learned to appreciate their genius with army rations very early.

We were in a tropical climate and malaria was prevalent. Everyone took atabrine tablets for a prophylaxis against the disease. Most of us developed severe diarrhea almost immediately. Officials ordered the practice discontinued when many became ill. They issued mosquito netting for our cots instead because the insect carried the parasite.

"What're you doing today?" I asked Danny a few days after we had arrived in Casablanca.

"Nothing special. Why?" she replied.

"Would you help me scrub the shower room? I don't feel clean after I use it because of the terrible smell."

We carried pail after after pail of water and scrubbed all afternoon. We found it impossible to remove the odor that had penetrated the cement for many years.

"We might as well give up," I said. "This is as clean as we'll get this shower stall." The stench was one of many unpleasant conditions we overlooked in the years ahead.

Most of us had a friend whom we had met on the ship from New York. We made many trips to the beach with these men because there was little else to do in Casablanca. The beaches were broad with low waves and gently breaking surf. I tried not notice the Arabs and their mangy camels and donkeys cooling off in the water a few feet away.

"I got a little sunburned today," I said to Mary when I returned to our quarters.

"Maybe you should watch it," said Mary. "We're closer to the equator than at home."

The next day Mary asked, "How'd you like to go to the roof with me to sunbathe? The sky is overcast so you shouldn't get burned."

We had been on the roof a short time when I said to Mary, "I'd better go. I feel hot and I think I'm burning."

A few hours later every inch of my exposed skin was brilliant red. I had fever and chills and felt nauseated. Mary got soda and vinegar from the mess hall and made a paste to cover my burns. I was in bed for several days before I recovered.

Our little brown books told much about bartering with the Arabs, but reading did not quite prepare us for the real thing. Our American money was exchanged for French francs. It was truly "filthy lucre," because the bills were all sizes and denominations, ragged and dirty. We could only guess what they were worth in American money.

Danny and I went into the main part of the city hoping to find something to buy. I searched all the small shops in the Place de la France and found a silver ring and two silver bracelets.

"The leather goods smell as bad as everything else," I said. "I'm not going to buy any of it. Let's go home."

We noticed men squatting on the street to relieve themselves. Danny said, "Let's take a carriage. I sure don't want to step in anything."

We got into one of the carriages waiting along the boulevard. About two blocks from our quarters, the driver stopped and demanded his pay. We offered five francs, but his gesturing clearly showed he wanted more. Danny filled his hand with coins.

"Let's go." She grabbed my hand and we ran toward home.

He shook his fist and shouted in Arabic. We ran until we were a safe distance away.

"Why was he so angry?" I asked Danny.

"Those coins were worth less than a franc. I just outsmarted an Arab."

We had a few parties in our mess hall while we were in Casablanca. Any flat surface served as a ballroom floor. All we needed was a record player for music. There were few American women and never a shortage of men for partners.

Gen. Fred Blesse, brother of our commanding officer, gave us some fatherly advice shortly after we arrived overseas. "Beware of the wolves," he said. "Figure out your code and stick to it."

After a party a short time later, guards found one of the nurses dumped inside the gate of the compound. She had been raped, and she was dazed and brutally beaten. Word of the crime traveled quickly throughout the area. The incident shocked everyone, both women and men. Authorities apprehended her assailant and scheduled him to stand trial by court martial.

With our sense of security shattered, we were cautious about going alone on dates for a while. The few that did venture out brought back the latest rumors; everyone hoped we would leave Casablanca soon.

The classrooms for the French children were on the ground floor of our quarters. I often stood at the window and watched the children play in the gravel play yard. They squealed and laughed while they jumped rope or played tag and other games I didn't recognize. They disappeared inside the building when they finished playing. We soon heard their childish voices singing the *Marseillaise*. The French children led an entirely different life from the Arab waifs we saw everywhere.

Our little brown books told of many Arab customs and we learned others by observation. We saw young boys with shaven heads except for small patches of hair on top. The hair was braided into a waist-length braid. This served as a handle to lift them from purgatory in case they died an untimely death. Another custom was to eat only with the right hand. They used the left for toilet and it was considered unclean. The Arabs did not drink any alcoholic beverages. Women did not show their faces in public.

I had been in Casablanca about a month when I received an invitation to dinner at the sultan's palace. Danny, two other nurses, and three of the doctors from the hospital also received invitations.

"I hope I don't get mixed up and use the wrong hand," said Danny.

"I wonder if the sultan lets any of his wives have dinner with us," I said. "This could be an interesting evening. At least we know no one will get drunk."

We rode through the crowded streets before reaching the palace on a hill overlooking the countryside. A stone wall covered with red bougainvillea surrounded the low, white buildings with red-tile roofs. Inside the wall were formal gardens of pink roses, red geraniums, purple gladiolas, and white lilies. Lemon and orange trees spread a soft fragrance throughout the garden. Palm trees towered overhead. There was only enough room to walk between the flowers on a narrow footpath.

The sultan, who had dark skin and dark eyes, stood about five-feet eight-inches tall. His snow white suit contrasted sharply with the colorful garden.

"Good evening," he said in perfect English. "I'm so glad you could come. Won't you come in?"

"He doesn't sound like an Arab to me," I whispered to Danny as we trailed the others single file through the garden.

We entered the palace through an arched entry decorated with Arabic tiles. The dining room had marble floors and white, overstuffed furniture against white walls. Skylights flooded the room with light. We seated ourselves at a low, round table surrounded by cushions six inches deep. I seated myself as gracefully as possible after watching others lower themselves to the floor cushions.

A barefoot Arab servant entered and placed a bowl of water, poured from a silver teakettle, in the center of the table. Everyone washed their hands because we would eat from a common bowl with our fingers.

The first course was chicken pot pie with almond paste. Next came a rack of roasted lamb. After a course of scrambled eggs with chicken livers, bread, and wine, I felt I'd had a full meal, but that was only the beginning. The following course was three roasted chickens with tart sour gravy. A pastry flavored with almonds came after the chicken. We had our first silverware for the next course. The servant brought a bowl of yogurt flavored with orange blossoms and we all ate from the same bowl. Dessert was oranges, the traditional dessert in Morocco.

"Did you see two women peek around the corner when we were leaving the room?" whispered Danny as we walked to the ballroom. Women and children never ate with male members of the household or appeared when there were guests in the house.

We went to the parlor after the meal and the sultan turned on the radio.

"That's Glenn Miller's band playing 'Manhattan Serenade!'" said Danny.

The officers in our group wanted to dance, so Danny and I each took a turn around the room. The servants brought coffee flavored with orange blossoms while we talked with the sultan.

We went to the music room where we met the sultan's son, who had attended Oxford University in England before the war. Music racks, a cello, a harp, and other large, stringed instruments surrounded the grand piano that almost filled the room. We had mint-flavored tea and cookies for the last course of the meal.

"It's getting late," I said to the others when I glanced at my watch. "We should go home."

We thanked our host for the memorable evening. A servant sprayed us with rose water from a large atomizer for good health and good fortune. We returned to our quarters and the real world of the army.

We were in Casablanca several weeks before we received mail from home. I continued to write regularly, although we could say little about where we were or what we were doing. The army censored the mail of enlisted personnel. Officers censored their own by signing their name across the front of the envelope. I sent a long uncensored letter home with a nurse who was returning to the States for health reasons. Home seemed a little closer after I tried to answer some of the questions I knew were on everyone's mind.

The war was going well for the Allied troops after many months of bitter fighting. We received word on May 12, 1943, that the Allies had defeated Hitler's Afrika Corps and the desert war was over. There was a big celebration in Casablanca the following Sunday. Troops paraded through the streets, followed by tanks, armored vehicles, and Jeeps filled with top military commanders. The sky overhead was full of planes—a show of strength by the air force. The question on our minds after the jubilant celebration was, what is ahead for us?

We received word at the end of May to be ready to proceed by truck convoy to Bizerte in Tunisia. This would be the first time the 56th had been together as a unit. The convoy consisted of 112 trucks in four sections of 32 trucks each. We were undaunted that only twenty men among the personnel had previous truck-driving experience. The trip would cover 1,300 miles over plains, mountains, and desert. Most trucks pulled a trailer loaded heavily with hospital supplies. The remaining trucks were for the nurses, their equipment, and personnel that did not drive.

"What are you going to wear?" I asked Mary.

"I'm wearing coveralls and sandals," she replied. "That's what everyone else is wearing."

We each filled our musette bag with books, playing cards, lipstick, Chapstick, writing supplies, cigarettes, and a towel.

"I'm going to put my dress uniforms in my bedroll," I said. "We won't need them on this trip. They'll be pressed when we get to Bizerte."

Mary reminded me, "Make sure you save enough room in your luggage for food. We'll each carry our own rations on this trip."

Our diet in Casablanca consisted of dehydrated potatoes, dehydrated eggs, fruit cocktail, Vienna sausages, powdered milk, Spam, and canned corned beef. I recalled the sumptuous meal at the sultan's palace and wondered if C rations would be an equally welcome change.

We assembled in front of the school to await the trucks to take us to meet the convoy at 0700 on June 4, 1943. Everyone dressed in olive-drab coveralls, brimmed hats, and sandals. We each wore a cartridge belt around our waist to carry a canteen with an aluminum cup and a mess kit. Morale was high and no one regretted leaving Casablanca.

"We're finally on our way," someone asked. "I wonder why we're going to Bizerte?"

"Maybe we're going there to join forces for an invasion of the continent," another answered.

The trucks arrived at 0900 hours. We rode to the assembling point for the convoy. We got our three tin cans of rations and one quart of water for the day. One meal of C rations consisted of corned beef hash, hardtack, and a powder for lemonade. The noon meal was meat and beans (which tasted like pork and beans), hardtack wafers, and lemonade powder. The last meal of the day was beef stew, hardtack, and lemonade. We ate our meals cold. Most of us did not drink the lemonade after we discovered that it made a much better hair rinse than it did a drink.

Ellen and Mary were among the twelve in our truck. We started the trip singing, "Over hill! Over dale! As we hit the dusty trail, the caissons go rolling along!" Natives crowded dangerously around the trucks as the convoy wound slowly out of the city.

The slat benches on each side of the truck bed furnished a place to sit. We rolled up the canvas sides for ventilation. The top shielded us from the intense sun. We often left the benches for a diversion and joined the non-stop card games.

Our destination the first day was Meknès by way of Rabat. We drove through coastal country dotted with prosperous French farms. Orange, lemon, and tangerine trees surrounded every home. Luscious melons, squash, sweet corn, and cabbages grew in the truck gardens. Arab peasant women with children strapped to their backs harvested grain with hand sickles. The men sat on smelly donkeys nearby and watched. Adults shoved children to the forefront to beg each time the convoy slowed.

We passed the beautiful city of Rabat, home of the sultans' principle palace, about noon. We stopped a few miles east of the city for a rest room break and lunch. An advance detail dug a trench six inches wide, two feet deep, and six feet long for a latrine. They surrounded the trench with canvas.

"It feels good to stretch my legs," I said to Mary as I jumped from the truck. "Let's hurry to the latrine before the others get there."

"Those C rations will taste good," said Mary. "Breakfast at five o'clock this morning was a long time ago." We sat on the ground near the truck to eat our can of cold meat and beans.

We arrived at our bivouac area in a broad, flat valley east of Meknès about dusk. Ward tents, with thirty cots in each tent, furnished shelter for the night. We had two blankets and a bare cot for each night of the trip. The water in our canteens warmed in the sun. We poured it into our helmets and washed the grime from our faces before falling asleep.

We started singing as soon as the trucks started to roll each morning. Our first tune was always the Army Hymn. We composed parodies to our favorite tunes, adding a verse each day, when we couldn't think of anything else to sing. Some of the these songs were lengthy by the time we reached Bizerte eight days later.

We traveled through fertile valleys filled with ripening grain and a kaleidoscope of bright wildflowers. Nestled among the low hills was the ancient Arab city of Fez. Its picturesque spires and minarets graced the skyline. We met a long convoy of American soldiers returning to the rear after combat in Tunisia. Fatigue showed in their faces, but they were in good spirits. There was a chorus of whistles and shouts when they saw women in the trucks.

"Say something!" they shouted. "We want to hear a woman that speaks English."

"Where will the next fighting be?" someone asked.

"Sicily," came the answer as the convoy moved past.

The landscape became more desert-like as we approached Gercif, where we would spend the night. The dust stuck to our faces in the dry, hot breezes. The water in the canteens was too hot to drink.

"Look, there's a river!" someone exclaimed. "Maybe we'll stop close enough for us to get a bath."

We dashed for the little stream as soon as we were off the trucks. Arabs watered their donkeys and camels on the opposite bank while we washed the dust and grime from our naked bodies.

"I think they're getting their eyes full," said Danny.

"Who cares?" I replied. "We'll never see them again."

Everyone turned in early and I never slept better than after the cool dip in the river. We traveled to Tlemcen the next day.

The trip took us through rich farmlands and orchards of cherries, lemons, and figs. Our stop for the night was in a broad, green valley at the foot of high mountains. A race track bordered our bivouac area.

I met Danny and said, "Let's walk around the tents a few times. That truck bed is getting smaller each day and I need some exercise."

"Me too," she replied. "Besides, I'd like to get away from some of the bitching in our truck for a while."

When we prepared to leave camp the next morning, we were treated to an unexpected spectacle. The race track filled with two hundred French cavalry. Men in their flowing red robes, plumed hats, and silver swords put their white steeds through precision drills. The show put everyone in high spirits for the grueling day ahead. Our fourth day on the road took us to Orleansville, two hundred miles away.

We traveled over high mountains not unlike the Rockies. Paved roads, in good condition, did not have guard rails, and we often found ourselves leaning toward the inside when we rounded a curve. Many times there was about three feet between the outside wheel and a precipitous drop of one to two thousand feet. We took advantage of the long daylight hours and got to camp late and left early. We reached the bivouac area at 2130 hours. I washed my face with cold water, took off my shoes, and fell into bed. We broke camp the next day at 0530 hours.

I tired of the card games and often sat and took in the scenery of the ever-changing landscape. The French owned the rich farmland. Arabs lived on the edge of the desert in mud shacks. Broad fields of grain and a profusion of flowers were everywhere. We passed fruit orchards and large groves of olive trees and nut trees. We tired of the monotonous diet of C rations. No one dared take the risk of eating native fruit and vegetables without a proper way to prepare them.

We rode through high mountains most of the next day. The trucks ground up the steep slopes over tortuous roads before reaching the summit. We held our breath as we rounded curves and could see nothing but space below us. Our home for the night was in an orange grove at L'Arba.

We rolled up the sides of the tent because it was a warm night. I heard planes nearby and discovered we were about a half block from the runway of a big airfield. The ground shook as the bombers roared down the runway. They lifted off when they were even with our tent. Wave after wave of these giants, with ten planes in each wave and a crew of ten on each plane, were on their way to bomb German installations. I fell into troubled sleep wondering how many planes would return and how many men would lose their lives.

We passed through many Arab villages the next day on our way to Setif. Natives crowded the street in every little hamlet to sell their wares. If the convoy slowed, even in remote area of the countryside, Arabs popped out of the ground. They crowded around the truck and scrambled for every thing we threw to the them.

"You can tell the Americans have been here," I said to Mary. The children begged for bon bons and gum.

We met long columns of German prisoners on their way to a port city for evacuation to England or the United States. Only a few American soldiers guarded as many as a thousand prisoners. We were envious that they would go to the States while our toughest days lay ahead.

It was stork-nesting time around Setif. It amused us to watch these awkward birds light on their crude nests that topped every chimney.

"How do they keep their young from falling from those nests?" we wondered.

We tired of C rations, no baths, slit-trench latrines, and the same clothing every day. The slat benches seemed harder and the truck bed smaller each mile we traveled. We searched for activities to amuse ourselves. Even those with the sunniest dispositions showed strain from the long trip.

We spent the last night in beautiful high-mountain country near Souk Ahres. Tomorrow would be our last day of travel and we expected to be in Bizerte before nightfall.

Morale was high when we prepared to climb aboard the trucks on the last day of our memorable journey. Arabs swarmed over the camp searching for anything we might leave behind. They examined the C-ration cans for any scraps of food clinging to the sides.

We had not gone far when we saw evidence of the bitter fighting that had just ended. The land was barren and desert-like. Shell holes and bomb craters ripped the surface of the road. Wrecked tanks, burned planes, and abandoned vehicles were everywhere. Crude crosses marked the graves of Americans, British, and German soldiers. Bombs had recently leveled every hamlet. Allies called the road Messerschmidt Lane after all the bombing that occurred there. We passed a large desert hill with a crude wooden cross that read "Hill #609." I fought back tears because the last letter from home had brought news that my oldest childhood friend had lost his life there. He was a medic with the 34th Division of the Iowa National Guard.

The convoy slowly approached a broad stream. Bombs had destroyed the bridge and the rubble lay in the river. The trucks drove carefully down the steep bank and across to the other side. We stood and hung onto the sides of the truck to brace ourselves against the jarring of the rough riverbed. The truck groaned and churned as it scaled the bank on the other side. We sighed with relief after we had crossed safely.

We sighted an inland lake ahead of us, and the masts of ships soon came into view. We entered the outskirts of Bizerte, the most bombed city in North Africa. Bombs had struck every building, and the streets were full of craters. Ships of every description filled the harbor and many had suffered heavy damage. An umbrella of silver barrage balloons floated overhead. Engineers cleared mines from a narrow road through the city. Our convoy slowly wound its way up the hill to Camp Nador where we would set up our hospital. Everyone said a prayerful thanks that we had made our eight-day trip of 1,300 miles without a serious accident.

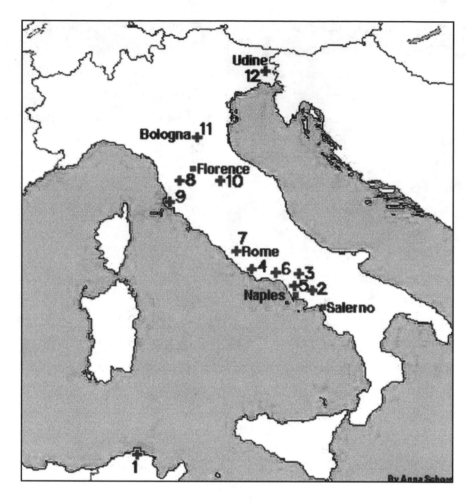

*Locations of the 56th Evacuation
Hospital in North Africa and Italy*

1. Bizerte 2. Avellino 3. Dragoni 4. Anzio
5. Caserta 6. Fondi 7. Rome 8. Peciolli
9. Piambino 10. Scarperia 11. Bologna 12. Udine

Chapter VII

Tunisia

Nurses' quarters were in the largest stucco building in the compound. Large dormitory-style rooms, surrounded by a balcony, were on second floor. The officers' and nurses' mess hall was on the ground floor. We did not look around much the first night. After cots were set up, no one wasted any time getting to bed.

Everyone was up early the next morning to look over our surroundings. Camp Nador was formerly a French garrison and had recently been occupied by the Germans. We had a grand view of Lake Bizerte on the west, the Mediterranean on the north, and east and below us was Bizerte and the village of Ferryville. The one story buildings were ideal for a hospital and we were finally going to be functioning as a unit. First on the agenda was hot showers for everyone.

One of the long buildings became a shower room. The nurses had thirty minutes for everyone to shower. A long pipe with a shower head every two feet made it possible for all of us to shower at the same time. The latrine, with canvas sides and a tarpaulin roof, had six holes and was behind the nurses' quarters. Even these accommodations seemed luxurious compared to slit trenches and no showers for the past eight days.

"I forgot how good it feels to be clean," I said to Mary after we showered.

"I hate you with that curly hair," she replied. "You don't need to do anything to it and it still looks great." We walked slowly back to our quarters soaking up the bright, warm African sun.

A trailer brought potable water to camp. After filling our canteens, we stored them under our cots for toothbrushing and washing our faces. We ran down stairs and behind the building to brush our teeth. We used water sparingly, hoping to save enough to do laundry in our steel helmets.

The buildings were filthy. They needed to be cleaned before we used them for a hospital. It was a monumental task to remove all the trash. Officers and men worked for a week clearing the buildings. They were full of garbage, guns, gas masks, bottles, and cans left behind by the Germans. Along with the rubbish, every kind of bug infested the buildings. The 175th Engineers were in the area a few weeks ahead of us and helped with the cleanup. The nurses had a few days off to rest after the trip.

I was lying face down on my cot hoping to get a little nap. I heard one of the nurses muttering and cursing when she tramped through our quarters. She carried a pail of water.

"What's the problem?" I asked.

"Bedbugs. My mosquito net is full of bedbugs," was her curt answer.

I thought, momentarily, *I'm glad it isn't mine.* I turned onto my back. I looked up and saw thousands of bugs on the olive-drab mosquito net. I quickly tore the netting from the cot, ran downstairs, and lit a match to it.

We slept under mosquito nets because malaria was very common in the area. I went to the supply tent for a replacement.

"Where's the one you're turning in?" the sergeant asked.

Operating room building at Bizerte

"I don't have one. I burned it," I replied.

"Can't you even find a piece of it? I'm sorry, but I can't issue another without a part of the first one."

I left filled with consternation. How would I get another net? Would I get malaria?

I walked slowly towards my quarters. I met Jon.

"Hi," he said. "How's it going?"

I related my problem with the bugs and the difficulty getting a replacement for the net.

"Don't worry," he assured me. "I know how to get you one." Jon brought a mosquito net few days later.

We experienced our first red alert soon after we arrived in camp. Fright and chilling alarm gripped me when two German planes flew overhead at 1900 hours. Even though they were barely visible in the bright evening sun, I realized we were in the thick of war. The harbor was full of ships. They, along with antiaircraft on shore, fired at the two tiny silver specks. The planes quickly disappeared into the evening sky beyond the hills. The reconnaissance planes did not drop any bombs.

We expected the fighting to start in Sicily soon because our air force was bombing the island. A large concentration of men, supplies, and ships surrounded Bizerte. Troops were alerted for action.

The buildings were soon cleaned with a lot of help from the 175th Engineers. They were glad to see American women and gave a party for the nurses before we opened the hospital. I met Jack Rafferty at the party and we became good friends for the rest of my time overseas. Jack always came by when his unit was in the same area as the 56th Evac.

The girl who was a rape victim and two nurses who had served as witnesses returned to camp following the court martial. They flew from Casablanca and all of us greeted them warmly.

"Was he found guilty?" everyone asked.

"I don't want to talk about it," said one of the witnesses, and started to cry.

The other witness volunteered, "He was acquitted of all charges. The trial was more brutal for Lonnie [the victim] than the rapist." We could not understand the verdict, since the evidence was so strong.

The officers and nurses had a party in our mess hall the night before everyone reported for duty. Lonnie left the party for a few minutes to return to our quarters. On the way back to the party, she missed a step in the dark and fell to the bottom of the stairs. She suffered a few cuts and scrapes but no serious injuries. We were bewildered and saddened when officials decided Lonnie was a liability and sent her back to the United States.

Someone started the rumor that Colonel Blesse was going to make a "bed check" of the nurses the next night.

"He wouldn't dare!" was the cry from everyone.

All of us were getting ready for bed when the door of our dorm opened. A sergeant stepped inside and shouted "Attention!" Colonel Blesse appeared in the doorway, obviously quite drunk. I grabbed a blanket and covered myself without getting off my cot. He went from cot to cot trying to say something pleasant to each of us. He received only cold stares. The sergeant escorted him quietly from our quarters. The executive officer advised him not to repeat the practice. All the nurses hummed the popular tune "Don't Fence Me In" the next day.

We reported for duty dressed in our blue seersucker dresses and white shoes on June 18, 1943. Nurses and officers with the 56th on maneuvers in Louisiana provided leadership in setting up the wards. We opened a packing box for a desk, another for medicine and supplies, and set up cots.

"Where are the sheets?" I asked. "I'll make up the cots."

"We don't use sheets," was the reply.

Each cot had a thin, cotton-filled mattress and two blankets. We covered every cot with a mosquito net. I thought about the many hours spent as a student nurse learning to make a proper bed. Here, we did not have square corners, carefully folded spreads, and plump pillows.

The hospital opened officially on June 20. The first patient was one of our own personnel. Nick had sandfly fever, a tropical disease, never seen before by our doctors. They treated his symptoms and he fully recovered in a week. Patients arrived in large numbers and the hospital soon filled to overflowing.

I worked on the medical service and saw some of the sickest men I'd ever seen. Malaria patients with violent chills followed by temperatures as high as 107 degrees were common. One young soldier shook so hard I thought the cot would surely break. We did not have hot-water bottles to break the chill. We added a few drops of water to a six-inch-square bag of chemicals. We kneaded the bag to create a chemical reaction that produced heat. There was a hazard of burns, but I had no time to think about that. I piled on blankets and tucked them around his violently shaking body. The soldier's chill subsided shortly and I took his temperature. It was 109 degrees. He started to cry and my own eyes filled with tears, making it hard to find the aspirin. I gave him a dose of aspirin and bathed his burning body with tepid water. His condition improved and we evacuated him to a station hospital a few days later. We had many of these cases. I don't know of any that did not survive, because they were in top physical condition.

There were frequent air raids over the port of Bizerte. The town was several miles away so we did not take them too seriously. We were jarred awake at 0300 hours on July 6 when planes roared overhead. Heavy gunfire boomed and crashed around us. We dashed to the balcony and saw the entire area bathed in a greenish white light. Flares dropped from planes overhead hung momentarily in the night sky and lit the entire area brighter than day. Red tracer bullets fired by antiaircraft guns around us filled the sky. Ships in the harbor sent booming salvos from their heavy guns toward the planes. Searchlight beams laced the sky. The spectacle was the most awesome fireworks we had ever seen. We heard the chilling scream of falling bombs and the explosive thud when they hit the earth.

"They've got one in the lights!" we shouted. "Get him! Get him!"

We watched the hapless German spiral toward earth, leaving a trail of smoke behind. We cheered as if we were at a sporting event. The raid lasted for more than an hour. Soon ambulances bringing the wounded lined the road leading to the hospital. We learned later that there were two hundred German planes in the raid. The hospital received more than two hundred wounded men. We'd had our baptism of fire.

We had another heavy raid two nights later. We grabbed our helmets and crouched together in the middle of the building. We learned quickly that air raids were not a spectator sport. The rat-a-tat-tat of antiaircraft guns and the explosive bursts of the heavy guns told us that bombs were falling in the area. Following the screech of falling bombs, we heard the tinkle of metal and dirt on the tile roof. We explored the area after the all clear sounded.

A German plane fell about one hundred yards from our building and there were bomb craters all around us.

A few days later, I saw one of the corpsmen (ward attendants) showing two well-worn gold rings to another soldier. One had a ruby set and the other a heavy, carved wedding band.

"Where'd you get those?" I asked.

"I took them from the pilots of the plane that fell near the nurses' quarters," he answered.

"We do not take items of a personal nature," I reminded him.

"I was there first, so they're mine now," was his reply.

I thought about our American men and wondered how the Germans treated them.

Bob Hope, Frances Langford, Tony Romano, and Jack Pepper came to the hospital to entertain us while were having heavy air raids. Men from surrounding installations and the hospital personnel gathered in front of the makeshift stage. All patients—the ambulatory, and those who could only get there with help—joined the crowd. Everyone sat together in the warm morning sunshine. They gave a wonderful show and we gave the troupe an enthusiastic welcome. Each of us felt a little closer to home.

We continued to have air raids while Bob Hope was in Tunisia. It was dangerous for Bob Hope and Company to stay in Bizerte. The harbor area around Bizerte was a primary target for the Germans. They stayed at our hospital while entertaining other military installations in the area. Red crosses marked the hospital and it was not a military target.

I was on night duty and Jon came over almost every evening. He brought the latest news and asked if I needed anything. I learned he was married. He knew everyone because he helped organize the 56th. Jon worked in the receiving ward.

He came one evening after a heavy raid the night before.

"Is Bob Hope still here?" I asked.

"He won't be back after last night," he said

"What happened? Was he wounded?" I asked.

"He came in the receiving tent last night after the raid. Wounded men were on litters everywhere. He thought his presence would boost their morale. Major McCauley didn't see it that way."

"What did he say?" I said.

Many went to see how many wounded were coming in when Major McCauley shouted, "Whoever isn't working in here, get the hell out! Dammit, I mean you too, Hope." Bob Hope left quietly to spend the rest of the evening with Colonel Blesse.

We received mail but little news about the progress of the war. We had a public address system for bugle calls, announcements, and messages. The men in headquarters decided we should start our own radio station. The station started operation on July 10, the day the Sicilian campaign started. They reported news from the *Stars and Stripes,* played music, reported sports, and did a little advertising. The broadcast started with "San Antonio Rose" and "The Eyes of Texas."

"I wonder if those songs have replaced the national anthem," I said to Ellen.

"We might as well get used to it, because we'll hear them often," she replied.

The station prospered in popularity, and patients and staff paused to listen to the evening broadcasts. Many from surrounding installations heard about the station and enjoyed the programs with us. I met Capt. Bob Marks when he came to listen. He was another faithful friend until the end of the war.

The broadcasts started by saying, "This is Station G.I. Camp Nador operating on any frequency." The soldier announcing proceeded to identify the sponsor: "Happy Chappy Macerated Corned Beef made from ten-year-old Texas steers."

We functioned as a unit after only few weeks of operation as a hospital. We began to think of ourselves as seasoned veterans.

Our chief nurse, Marguerite Ray, was a shy, insecure woman in her middle thirties. She confided that she was very unhappy being in charge because of so many strong personalities among the nurses. We had been in Bizerte a short time when she quietly left the 56th. Her replacement was Capt. Dorothy Meadors, a popular choice. Captain Meadors, in her middle forties, was also quiet and soft-spoken. She was fair and exerted strong leadership.

Hospital ships arrived in the Bizerte harbor daily with wounded from the fighting in Sicily. We had American, British, Italian, and German patients. One group of Americans was especially bitter about their wounds. They were paratroopers flown in to support ground forces invading Sicily from the sea.

"Our own navy shot us down," said a captain bitterly. He had both legs in casts and many shell fragments still in his body.

"Maybe they couldn't tell they were American planes," I said, trying to ease his bitterness.

"We were flying low in C-47s. Any idiot should be able to tell them from enemy planes."

A German captain, a member of the elite Nazi S.S. troops, was a patient on my ward. He had a severed sciatic nerve. I found him perspiring and with a wild look in his eyes that left little doubt that he was in excruciating pain. I got a syringe of morphine and tried to show I would give him a shot for pain.

"Nein! Nein!" he shouted, and drew back his fist as if to strike me.

One of the nurses on the ward spoke German. I asked her to explain what I planned to do.

He believed the German propaganda that said we killed the wounded with drugs rather than treat them. He took the shot reluctantly.

We heard about young Gen. George Patton who led the troops so brilliantly in North Africa. We knew he was in Sicily. The officer on my ward called the nurses and wardmen together shortly after the fighting started there.

"I want to remind you that we give our finest care to everyone," he said. "It does not matter if they are American, other allies, civilians, or prisoners. I just heard that General Patton slapped a patient at a hospital in Sicily." Everyone gasped in disbelief. "No one in this organization will tolerate such behavior. Also remember that you must never take anything of personal nature from a prisoner. This includes pictures, billfolds, and jewelry." I thought about the ward attendant with the two gold rings.

We often heard the drone of our planes approaching in the crystal-clear morning sky. Slowly the planes came into view, ten big bombers in each wave, flying in formation. Fighter planes flitted among them like shepherd dogs trying to keep the flock together. Wave after wave of B-17 bombers, P-38s, and P-51s were on their way to unload bombs in daylight raids over Germany. We watched for their return in the afternoon. Some of the planes were missing from the formations. Others had holes in the fuselage and many had still props. We dared not think of what happened to many of our airmen.

Our camp began to look like a military installation. Rocks lined walks and flower beds. Purple, pink, and red flowers surrounded every stucco building. The PX was open but there was little to buy. The army issued toothpaste, soap, gumdrops, cigarettes, and hard candies. We received Hershey bars specially developed to prevent melting. They did not melt in the hot African sun or when heated over fire.

The war ended in Sicily after thirty-eight days of fighting. We expected to leave our first hospital site soon. The administration furnished trucks for us to make a trip to the ancient city of Carthage. We walked among the ruins of antiquity and marveled at how well they had lived in Biblical times.

We saw a bathtub that looked like one at home and wished we could take it with us.

The 24th General Hospital came to take over our hospital on September 17. We moved into tents in a bivouac area near Bizerte. Everyone had a rumor concerning our destination. Would we be going to England? France? Or maybe even home? The answer came once more in two little brown books. One was called *Soldier's Guide to Italy* and the other *Italian Words and Phrases*. We learned that we would sail for Italy on September 25 and arrive on Sunday, September 26.

The Italians surrendered to the Allies while we camped in the bivouac area. Would Italy be a grand sightseeing tour?

"I hope we get to Rome," said Mary.

"Maybe we'll have a chance to do some Christmas shopping before we're sent somewhere else," I said. "I'd like to do some traveling. There's a lot to see in Italy."

We received K rations, developed for short-term use, for the boat trip. They consisted of a one-and-one-half-ounce tin of processed cheese, two round hardtack crackers, lemonade mix, and two pieces of hard candy. Also included were a few sheets of toilet paper. The rations were convenient and adequate because it was a short trip to Italy.

The nurses would make the trip on LCI (Landing Craft Infantry) #238. These craft drew little water so they could sail close to the beach and allow infantry to wade ashore. We boarded the ship and waited to start our trip. Orders were slow coming, so some of the nurses jumped off the side of the ship and went swimming. I looked on enviously at Ellen and Mary swimming in the suits they had bought in New York. Others fashioned swim suits from pajamas, shorts, and bandannas.

Word came to set sail. We had not gone far before we knew it would be a rough ride. It was hot and everyone was in one cabin below deck. Our cabin filled with fumes from the motor and the sea was rough. We did not go far before seasickness claimed its first victims. We saw Camp Nador, on the hill above Bizerte, fade in the sunset. No one regretted leaving North Africa. Every move meant we were closer to the end of the war.

"Let's sleep on the top deck," I said to Danny. "It's too hot down below."

We looked around on the upper deck, casting eerie shadows in the light of a full moon.

"Looks like this is about the best place," said Danny. We found a spot four feet wide and four feet long. "We can use that coil of rope for a pillow."

"Let's stand up and stretch," I said to Danny during the night. It was hard to straighten up after a few hours on the steel deck. We hung onto the two ropes that prevented us from slipping overboard into the rough sea.

We awoke to bright sunshine. The vague outline of hills and ancient Greek temples appeared on the horizon. We were approaching the shores of Italy.

We sailed into the midst of a large convoy anchored offshore. A white hospital ship glistened in the sun outside the circle of ships. A few British barrage balloons floated overhead.

We watched the LST (Landing Ship Tank), a much larger ship than an LCI, with our officers and men, approach the beach and unload. The men held their packs high above their heads while they waded ashore.

The end of our ship opened and we lined up for our turn to land. I was near the end of the line. I watched those ahead of me, with musette bag held above their heads, step into the shoulder-deep water. A line of soldiers on each side prevented anyone from slipping below the surface. I looked around for my musette bag and realized I had left it below deck. I ran back to retrieve it and then hurried back to my place in line. An army duck (amphibious truck) arrived to take the rest of the nurses ashore. Many were already on land, but I gladly accepted the ride and arrived in Italy safe and dry.

Chapter VIII

Avellino

We landed near Pasteum, a small village a few miles south of Salerno. We crossed the heavily mined beach on a carefully marked path between two lines of soldiers. After the pitching, rolling LCI, the ground was unsteady and I staggered until I recovered my equilibrium. A truck waited to take us three miles inland where we spent the next few days.

The 95th Evac landed the day before we reached Italy. They treated us to warm food and coffee.

I saw Gertrude Morrow, and asked, "How was your trip?"

"Outside of getting scared half to death," she said, "it was fine. We came over on a hospital ship."

"I hope it was more luxurious than the LCI we came on," I replied.

"Oh, it was! We had beautiful rooms and food like at home. The Germans bombed the ship last night. It terrified us. Two bombs hit the ship but, thankfully, they didn't injure anyone." I felt ashamed that I had mentioned our rough voyage.

"You can have our cots tonight," said Gertrude. "After two nights on an LCI, you need a bed. We'll sleep on the ground."

We awoke the next morning to warm temperatures and bright sunshine. The men unloaded the ships and all supplies and personnel gathered in a field a few miles from the beach. The kitchen sprang into action and we had a meal of warm C rations. After a few days of K rations, anything warm was a treat. While standing in line for our food, it gave us a chance to talk to the officers and men of our outfit. We compared notes on our trip from Africa and heard the latest rumors. We also wondered why we were in Italy if the Italians had surrendered. We took our food and sat on the ground to eat. We washed our tin mess kits and cups in steaming barrels of soapy water and rinsed them in another.

Our camp was in a beautiful setting despite being in a potato field. Steep mountains with tiny villages clinging to their sides surrounded us. Villagers in ancient times could see an approaching enemy from this precarious location and could defend themselves better.

The nurses spent the next few nights in ward tents. We expected to be here only a short time and no one minded living with twenty-five others. Mary and I would be tent mates and Ellen and Lena would share a tent when we moved into two-person tents. Italian civilians swarmed around the fringes of the camp eager to sell *vino,* nuts, and fruit. They took anything offered to them, especially cigarettes and chocolate.

Lena had a friend, Whitey, who was in the x-ray department and was a buddy of Jon.

"Whitey and Jon want us to meet them tonight," said Lena. "They have a bottle of wine and want to celebrate our arrival in Italy."

"Find out where we're supposed to meet and come by when you're ready to go," I replied.

We stumbled across the potato patch and found a downed tree where we met to drink our wine.

"This wine is terrible. The Italians must have made it yesterday."

"It's pretty bad, I agree," said Jon.

"I'm happy to be in Italy and away from those air raids. They age a person in a hurry."

"I won't miss the Arabs and the awful smell of North African cities," offered Lena.

We soon noticed flashes of lightning followed by the rumble of thunder.

"We'd better get back to our tent," I said to Lena. "It looks like we're going to have a storm."

We raced back to our tent amid blinding lightning and the constant crash of thunder. The wind came up in hurricane force about the time we reached our tent. The canvas flapped wildly in the wind and offered little protection. I gathered my personal belongings under my cot to keep them dry in the torrential rain. Everyone held the sides of the tent to keep it from collapsing in the wind. We heard screams from the adjoining tent and knew their shelter had blown down, so we shared our tent with the unfortunate victims for the remainder of the night.

Daylight dawned without a cloud in the sky. The sight that greeted us was a disaster area. Tents were down, belongings scattered, and everything was floating in a sea of mud.

We spent much of the next day trying to get some order into our living conditions. Tent ropes were full of soggy clothing and we spread bedding and mosquito nets on tent tops to dry in the sunshine.

I saw Danny later in the day and she said, "The colonel is furnishing a truck for a trip up the mountain. We should go. It'll give us a good view of the area and that's better than sitting here in the mud."

Ten of us met at 1430 hours for the trip. The open truck climbed slowly over narrow roads, switchbacks and hairpin curves. Clouds rolled in and we were soon above them. We shivered in the cool mist that enveloped the truck. Hollow-eyed children along with men and women in tattered black clothing were in every doorway in the tiny village. The people were hungry and we wondered how they existed. The children eagerly accepted the few pieces of hard candy we had with us. The only food supply we could see was a few scrawny chickens. The stone houses were set close to the street without sidewalks. The driver jockeyed the truck back and forth to turn it around. The view coming down the mountain was breathtaking. We saw the beach and the deep blue Mediterranean beyond through a break in the clouds. Near the beach were the ancient ruins of Pasteum and the Greek temple of Diana, goddess of the moon.

We returned to camp at dinner time. We had an unexpected treat of real potatoes and fresh tomatoes from nearby fields for dinner: our first fresh vegetables in several months.

Naples fell on October 1 after bitter fighting. We received orders for our next assignment, which was in Avellino, forty miles inland and southeast of Naples.

We traveled over some of the most spectacular scenery in southern Italy. The narrow, winding mountain roads went through villages with streets barely wide enough for the trucks to pass. Ragged children and pale adults watched as the convoy drove through the rubble-strewn villages. We tossed candy, crackers, and gum when the trucks slowed. The children grinned broadly while they scrambled to gather their loot and begged for more.

It was harvest season in the vineyards on the lower elevations. The vines were full of clusters of purple and white grapes. The Italian farmers gathered the crop for wine.

Every village had suffered severe damage from the fighting. Stone farm buildings used by the Germans for outposts, and later by the Americans, were a pile of rubble. Wrecked vehicles, both German and Allied, filled the landscape. Roads were full of holes and the Germans blew all the bridges when they retreated farther north. The air had a heavy odor of decaying flesh from bodies still unburied in Avellino. We reached our hospital site, Scuola Allievi Ufficiali (former government buildings), on the outskirts of town about noon.

We unpacked our equipment and began to set up the hospital immediately. Our air force had made a direct strike on every building in the quadrangle. None of the bombs struck the stairs, so we were able to get our equipment to the second floor.

Two soldiers swept hand grenades with a broom and someone stopped them before any detonated. A gust of wind blew out a window and it struck one of the nurses in the head. The blow dazed her, but she suffered no serious injuries. We soon had the hospital open in spite of these mishaps.

Receiving admitted three hundred patients, most of them wounded in combat, by midnight. Soldiers arrived at the hospital caked with mud and unshaven and they had the appearance of old men. The infantry suffered wounds much worse than those we saw from air raids in Bizerte. Our 750-bed hospital soon swelled to 1,100 patients. The buildings could not hold all the wounded. Our men set up tents to handle the overflow. Most of the casualties did not have just one wound but suffered multiple fractures from the shrapnel of bursting shells. The most critically wounded went to surgery first, and our surgeons operated around the clock. Those with less serious injuries had their wounds cleaned and casts applied. We evacuated them to a station hospital in the rear for further surgery.

Mary and I lived together in a two-person tent. We rarely saw each other because she worked in surgery. I worked on a ward filled to capacity with medical patients. Some suffered from malaria and upper respiratory infections. Others had venereal diseases and needed treatment before they returned to battle.

Morale was good among the wounded. They knew they would not go back to the front lines of fighting. Ambulatory patients fed those that needed a hand, carried urinals, and helped others shave.

A handsome six-foot four-inch sergeant with a sprained ankle was especially helpful around the ward. "I think you're ready to go back to your outfit, don't you?" said the ward officer. "I hate to see you go. You've been such good help around here."

On the ward two days later, there was a makeshift screen of blankets around a cot.

"Who's behind the screen?" I asked.

"We have a seriously wounded patient we'll evacuate this morning," said the night nurse.

I went to the cot and saw the sergeant we had discharged two days earlier. I did not recognize him for a few moments. Bandages swathed his traumatically amputated arms. His face, including his eyes, was full of steel fragments. He had suffered the wounds when a hand grenade exploded in his hands. The sight of this cruelly wounded man sickened me. I did not know if I could go on, but knew I had to.

Our hospital serviced troops in the Fifth Army commanded by Gen. Mark Clark. The Fifth Army had several divisions, among them the 34th, a National Guard division from Iowa and Minnesota. Other divisions were the 36th from Texas and the 45th Thunderbird Division from Oklahoma. Many other units, including armored divisions, ranger battalions, and paratroopers, were part of the Fifth Army. We were not in Italy long before we knew our hearts were with the infantry.

The fighting was fierce when our troops tried to cross the Volturno River. The Germans blew the bridges across every stream and ravine in the treacherous mountain terrain. The difficult task of getting ammunition and rations added to the infantryman's misery. Piles of blood-soaked, mud-caked clothing was outside the receiving tent every morning. The soldiers took cover in barns and often suffered their wounds in these buildings. Barnyard smells clung to the clothing. I got a clear sense of horror these men had endured when I walked through the wards. Everyone talked about their good fortune because they were only wounded instead of killed. The missile "didn't have my name on it."

Soldiers referred to the enemy as Jerries or krauts. The British were limeys and the American soldier was a yank or a G.I. Some called the infantryman a "dog-face."

All personnel lived in canvas tents while we were in Avellino. We were in a blackout area and did not have electricity. The tent Mary and I shared was about eight feet by eight feet and everyone enjoyed the privacy of only one roommate.

Our steel helmets were invaluable for laundry basin or bath basin. Rayon underwear hung several days on a string across the tent before it dried.

"I'm going to look for a laundry woman the next time we move," I said to Mary.

"I'll ask one of the enlisted men in surgery to find us one," said Mary. "They're good at making contacts."

We enjoyed the luxury of a laundry woman a few days later.

We had church services regularly for those who could get away from duty to attend. A small electric organ was among the hospital supplies. One of our surgeons, Major Willis, was an accomplished organist.

"Let's go to chapel," I said to Lena.

"Major Griffen's sermons don't inspire me," she replied. "I love the music Major Willis gets from the organ, though."

"It's too bad Captain Printy [the Catholic chaplain] isn't chaplain for all denominations," I said. "You see him on the wards at all hours of the night."

"I know," said Lena. "If I need someone, I call Captain Printy even if the patient isn't Catholic."

Chapel was in the mess tent and we sat on six-inch boards supported by hollow tiles. Thirty-five enlisted men, ten nurses, and six officers gathered for the morning services. We sang "Jesus Savior, Pilot Me" and "What a Friend We Have In Jesus" with more feeling than I had ever known.

"It felt good to be in chapel," I said to Lena. "The war hasn't changed the hymns. They are about the only thing that's the same."

Our diet consisted mainly of C rations. Italians came by camp with hastily concocted wine. They discovered early the American's appetite for any kind of liquor. An Italian came with candy bars made of burnt sugar and loaded with filberts. I bought some to satisfy my longing for something sweet.

"I've got a surprise for dessert tonight," I said to Mary when we left the mess hall.

"Did you buy some of the wine?" she asked.

"No, it's something even better," I answered.

We enjoyed every morsel of our rich, sweet treats. Both of us developed severe diarrhea before bedtime. We didn't know if it was from the unwrapped candy bars or that our systems couldn't stand the variety in our diet.

Word passed quickly a few days later that we would have fresh meat for dinner. The captain in charge of the mess bartered for a water buffalo from an Italian. We lined up early for dinner because no on wanted to miss the unusual treat. Bill, Paul, and Carl beamed as they gave each person their portion of the stringy red meat. We spared them listening to our gripes about the rations for one meal.

"It tastes a little like beef," I said to Mary.

"I'm afraid I'll break my teeth," she said. "It's so tough I can hardly chew it. I'll stick to C rations." Water buffalo did not become a staple in our diet.

Ward attendants carried rations to the wards in five- and ten-gallon metal containers. We served food on aluminum plates. Mealtime was always one of the busiest hours of the day, and for me, one of the saddest. While we sent all ambulatory patients to the patients' mess, there were those heavily encased in plaster who had to wait for someone to feed them. The meager rations were cold and unappetizing by the time it was the last man's turn for feeding. In spite of the shortcomings, no one complained.

Corporal Bucher was a corpsman who eagerly and cheerfully helped around the ward. I did not need to remind him it was time for meals, to bring water, or to help those in casts or any other task around the ward. I appreciated his helpful attitude.

When Corporal Bucher did not show up for duty one morning, I asked, "Where's Bucher?"

"He's on his way home," said the corpsman.

"How'd he manage that? Was there a death in his family?" I asked.

The soldier did not answer and shrugged his shoulders. I did not have time to question him further.

Jon came by later in the day. I said, "They sent Bucher home. Do you know why? I miss him."

He paused a short time before he answered. "He was homosexual and the army couldn't keep him."

I recalled Bucher proudly showing me a picture of his wife and two-year-old daughter. I was sorry to see him go home under these circumstances.

The bitter fighting continued while our troops tried desperately to cross the Volturno River. Our hospital was the first medical treatment many received. Some of the most critically wounded received emergency treatment in a field hospital, where they started plasma. Medics gave doses of morphine in the field and every soldier carried a packet of sulfa drugs to pour in his wounds. We had many suffering from severe bleeding, abdominal wounds, and sucking chest wounds. They always went to surgery first.

After a couple of weeks, the lines broke. The Germans retreated farther up the peninsula to fortify their lines. The stream of patients slowed. A sister evacuation hospital leapfrogged over us to service the troops.

We took advantage of the lull in the work and did some sightseeing in the area. We admired Monte Vergine, a monastery snuggled on the summit of the highest mountain above our camp. Those that visited it told of the incomparable view from the monastery.

I sat on my cot pondering how to take fullest advantage of a rare day off duty. The answer came when an announcement blared on the PA. "Lieutenant Dagit, please come to headquarters."

Captain Bill Marks greeted me and asked, "How'd you like to go to the monastery?"

"I'd love it!" I exclaimed. "I've been wanting to go up there."

It was a beautiful fall day with cool breezes and bright sunshine. We had gone only a short distance when we came to a steep ravine. The rubble that was once a bridge lay at the bottom.

"What do we do now?" asked Bill.

"Maybe we should go back," I said.

We sat a few minutes contemplating what we should do when Bill said, "Oh, I think we can make it."

The embankment appeared straight down and I hung onto the side of the seat. From the bottom of the ravine, the opposite embankment appeared even steeper. The car slipped backward as we tried to scale the other side. We finally made it to the top after three tries. When we were safely across, both of us sighed with relief.

"You know we'll have to go through this again on our way back," I reminded Bill good-naturedly.

We wound our way higher and higher over hairpin curves before reaching the summit. We had a panoramic view of Naples. Sunken ships filled the harbor. Mount Vesuvius, with a plume of smoke floating lazily from its peak, was in the background. Small villages dotted the mountainsides. Ancient Greek temples on the beach stood against a backdrop of the deep blue Mediterranean. Our hospital, with red crosses clearly visible, spread out in the valley below us.

The monastery was a cluster of bleak stone buildings and there was little evidence of creature comforts. Three pale young men in long brown robes greeted us.

"I'd like to buy a souvenir," I said, "but I can't see anything to buy here. We might as well go home."

We spent thirty minutes looking at the scenery before starting our trip down the mountain. I dreaded the return trip, but it went smoothly. I saw Bill many times in the next two years. He always mentioned how scared he was on the drive up the mountain.

Our troops crossed the Volturno and the flow of patients almost ceased. Everyone had their first chance to visit Naples. Bombs and shells had flattened all the buildings near the harbor. Old men and women peasants, in tattered black clothing, picked through the rubble. They looked for anything they could salvage. I tried to feel their misery and knew we were living well compared to their meager existence.

The army printed money for the armed forces. The bills had the same value as American bills and coins. Now we could tell what we paid for our purchases. Vendors were everywhere with cheap jewelry, cameos, rosaries, and wine. The cameos were inexpensive works of art when troops entered Naples. Prices escalated quickly and quality became questionable when the Italians discovered Americans yearning for souvenirs.

Danny and I visited Pompeii on a trip to Naples. Italians were eager to guide us through the ancient ruins. Mount Vesuvius erupted in A.D. 79 and buried the city and all the inhabitants with lava and ash. Chariot ruts were still visible in the streets. Many rooms were brothels and the artworks that decorated the walls were of questionable taste. One guide would not allow us, being women, to view some of the art.

"I want to see what he thinks is too vulgar for us to see, don't you?" said Danny. "I'll decide for myself."

We concluded, after interpreting his gesturing and Italian still mixed with a little German, that we could view the offensive pictures for ten lira (ten cents).

"What was all the fuss about?" I said. "I resent the fact we had to pay ten cents more than the men."

After viewing the art, brothels, and wine shops, we concluded that the early Romans had led a decadent life.

The hospital received word in early November to pack and prepare to move to Caserta. The Germans had moved farther up the peninsula, so the army cancelled the orders. We moved near the little town of Dragoni instead.

Chapter IX

Dragoni

We packed our belongings and the men struck the tents. There was no other place to sit, so we used our helmets for stools. We were up early to be ready because each move meant we were closer to home. Word finally came at 1000 hours that the trucks were loaded and we would leave at 1300 hours. The nurses traveled in open trucks for the forty-mile trip across the Volturno to a tiny village in a farming valley.

We started our usual singing , with Ellen leading, while the trucks slowly lined up in convoy. Morale was high. We talked optimistically of seeing Rome by Christmas. Dragoni was northeast of Naples and Rome was the next big prize.

We wound slowly around mountains on shell-pocked roads. The convoy slowed when we crossed the ravines on newly constructed bridges built by U.S. Army engineers. Women scrubbed laundry on the rocks at every mountain stream. Children played nearby and donkeys stood a few feet away. They all paused to stare when the convoy passed.

Military police stopped us a few miles down the road. They carefully guided each truck onto the pontoons that bridged the Volturno. I sat quietly and held my breath while the truck rumbled slowly to the other side. I reflected reverently on the heavy price our men had paid for the crossing.

We arrived at camp in time to set up tents before darkness fell. The farm families around the hospital site fled before we arrived. None of the homes were inhabitable. The burned-out wreckage of a German tank sat across from the entrance to the area. Sharply rising mountains surrounded us.

All personnel and the hospital were in tents for the first time. We were in a blackout area and did not doubt that the front was near. Fighting was fierce in the mountains a few miles away. We saw flashes of light and heard the rumble of the big guns when we fell asleep.

Our first two days in camp were beautiful without a cloud in the sky. The mountains had a lavender glow in the morning sun. Nothing predicted the coming changes in the weather.

The hospital was ready to receive patients on November 4. The weather started to change about the same time. Low clouds hung over the valley and there was a constant light drizzle. The drizzle turned to a steady downpour by the middle of the month. We marveled at the beauty of the Apennines when we came to Italy. Now they were an enemy, along with the rain, the cold, and the Germans.

Casualties were heavy and the wounded filled the hospital to overflowing. Surgery, once again, operated around the clock. Patients were mud-caked and blood-soaked. Several days' growth of beard did not hide their weary faces. Although most were in their twenties, they appeared much older.

Roads became quagmires. Ambulances churned through the mud to bring the wounded to the hospital. Litter bearers carefully negotiated ankle-deep puddles while carrying patients to the wards. Drops of water formed on the tops of the ward tents. We moved cots from one spot to another to

The mud was deep at Dragoni

get away from the steady drip. The olive-drab wool blankets were damp. Thin cotton-filled mattresses smelled musty, but no one complained. The wounded came to the hospital after many days in water-filled foxholes on freezing, craggy mountainsides. Ernie Pyle wrote that a tent felt good and a mattress was like so much velvet to an infantryman. Their wounds ended their fighting days for most of them.

"It's great to hear an American woman's voice," said a young soldier.

"You look just like my sister," said another.

"Could you sit here and talk?" said a soldier with casts on both arms and his leg. I sat on the edge of his cot.

"Where're you from?" I asked.

"Cedar Rapids, Iowa," said the soldier.

"I'm from Williams. That's a little town between Webster City and Iowa Falls," I said. "I have relatives in Cedar Rapids, the Leath family. Do you know them?"

"Sure. I was in high school with Dale."

I hoped that the few minutes we talked eased some of his pain, and both of us felt a little closer to home.

Daylight was shorter each day. Our tents were dark and damp and we did not have electricity.

"I'd love a place for a candle and to get my musette bag off the ground," I said to Mary.

"We should ask for ration boxes," said Mary. "I'll ask Bill or Paul for two. Many who have them say they're good bedside tables." Two days later Mary came to the tent with two boxes.

I undressed for bed on my cot. "I wish I could find a way to get in bed without filling my sleeping bag with mud," I said.

Mildew covered our barracks bags and the clothes inside smelled sour. We had given up wearing white shoes long ago. We no longer wore dresses because we needed olive-drab woolen shirts and pants for warmth. There was little to distinguish our dress from the men. The soupy mud was ankle deep in places and our galoshes offered little protection. Lizards and mice invaded our tents to escape the steady downpour.

It was cold. We saw the snow coming farther down the sides of the mountains when the clouds lightened a little. Each tent had a pot-bellied stove, but fuel was scarce. We found small amounts of wet wood, but it was a challenge to get a fire started. Mary and I tried every fire-starting method we heard about.

"Jon said the fire would start if we crumpled a lot of paper and laid small sticks on top," I told Mary.

We tried it, but the fire had flickered out when we lifted the lid of the stove.

"I still have some lighter fluid," I said. "Let's try that." We gave up and went to bed after trying for more than an hour without any luck.

Lts. Grussing and Dagit gathering firewood

An announcement came over the PA speaker the next day. "Attention, all personnel. You may pick up your ration of charcoal at the supply tent."

Mary and I tried again to get a fire started. We had even poorer luck with the charcoal. We used sticks, lighter fluid, and paper and ended up with a tent full of smoke. We saved two pages of the *Stars and Stripes* for fans to chase the smoke from the tent. When I emerged from the tent for a breath of air, I saw many from neighboring tents who had also been smoked out. The smoke clung to our clothing, blankets, and hair.

I was always cold in bed and my hips ached from lying in a rigid position.

"I could stand the rain and cold better if I could get a good night's sleep," I said to Jon when he came to the ward.

"Try putting more blankets under you and not so many on top," he suggested. "I can get you more blankets."

I folded four blankets lengthwise on top of my sleeping bag. I covered myself with five and slept soundly for the first time in many days.

We stood in line out of doors for our food. Rain ran from our hats and down our necks. The C rations floated in the water on our tin plates. Everyone had a wry remark about "sunny Italy." We ate our rations inside the mess tent.

The shower tent was cold and drafty. Mary and I resorted to baths from our helmets. We washed each other's backs and convinced ourselves we were clean and refreshed. Mary found an Italian woman to wash our clothes and that solved our laundry problem for the time being. The laundry came back spotlessly clean and pressed. We ignored the tiny holes burned in our shirts from sparks of the charcoal fires that the Italians used to heat their homes.

Engineers came with heavy equipment to grade away the thin mud on the main road. Officials hoped this would make a firmer base for ambulances. The success was questionable. Many loads of gravel were dumped on the main road and it quickly disappeared into the quagmire.

Our mail was irregular and often came in bunches. Mail from home was the greatest of all morale builders. Mary knew her father had surgery for cancer of the throat and was reportedly doing well.

I saw Ellen when she asked, "Have you talked to Mary since the mail came?"

"I haven't seen her since morning," I said. "Did she hear from home?"

"Sister Agnes wrote that she just returned from her father's funeral," she said. "Mary is taking it pretty hard."

Mary met Capt. Dick Smith while we were in Casablanca. They fell in love and planned to get married when the war was over. Dick came often, and I was grateful for his support of Mary during those dark days. Mary's letter shook my own sense of security. I received every letter with dread and joy for a while even though my parents were young and in good health.

The rain and cold brought patients with new problems. We received hundreds of men who had been sitting in foxholes filled with water. Many were unable to walk on their red, swollen feet when they reached the hospital. The condition was called "trench foot." We gave them dry socks, rest, and warm foot baths. We sent those that improved back to the front to continue fighting.

We eventually adjusted to living in these conditions. We dared not feel sorry for ourselves and believed that the war would end soon and everyone could go home.

Our mess tent had a wooden floor and just about anything was an excuse for holding a dance. One of our surgeons, Sam, loved to dance and I was his favorite partner. Sam and I became good friends and I felt safe and secure with him.

Many of the military groups in the area gave parties and invited the nurses. We made a special effort to attend any party given by the infantry. We understood the unbearable hardships they endured at the front.

We dressed in our best uniforms for the dances but found it impossible to look well groomed. We heard we would get new uniforms. Every speck of mud showed on navy blue and the new uniforms would be olive drab. The day arrived to be measured for them.

"It'll be like getting a whole new wardrobe," I said to Danny.

"I can hardly wait," she replied. "Olive drab will be closer to the color of mud."

A few days later, we received word that all officers and nurses would have five-day leaves on the Isle of Capri, "the Pearl of the Mediterranean." This was our first relief of duty since we came to Italy. The chief nurse divided us into two groups, because everyone could not leave at the same time. I watched enviously as Danny prepared to leave with the first group.

"I must lay this uniform carefully under me," said Danny as she brushed the specks of mud from her skirt. She placed it in her sleeping bag. "I want the creases to be in the right places. I sure wish we had our new uniforms."

"I'll count the days until it's my turn to go," I said. "We'll have to compare notes when we both get back."

Danny was gone and Mary was working the night shift. I was alone in the cold, dark tent and decided I would go to bed to stay warm. I put on the cozy flannel nightgown from Mother. She'd sent it after I complained in a letter home about being cold. I was dropping off to sleep when I heard a rap on my tent.

"Are you awake, Avis?" said Lena. "Could you come help me?"

I answered groggily, "What's the problem?"

"Ellen fell in the mud," she said, "and I don't know what to do."

I hated to get out of bed and, besides, all of us had problems with the mud.

"I'll come as soon as I find my shoes," I replied.

Ellen was standing in the middle of the tent. Soupy mud covered her from head to toe, except her face. She was quite drunk. I steadied her so she would not fall and get mud on her bed.

She said, "That son of a bitch ran over me three times."

"How could he do that?" asked Lena doubtfully.

"I fell out when we hit a bump and he ran over me," said Ellen. "He backed up and ran over me the second time. When he didn't see me, he drove ahead and that was the third time."

"Are you hurt?" I asked. "We'd better make sure you're not as soon as we get these clothes off."

Lena had a warm fire in her tent. I leaned over to remove Ellen's shoes.

"Do you smell something burning?" I asked.

"It's your gown," said Lena. "You brushed against the stove."

We threw Ellen's clothes outside the tent. "The rain will wash some of the mud off and she can turn them in tomorrow," said Lena, as we tucked Ellen into bed.

I kept the gown for the rest of my days overseas. I was grateful that the hole was only three by five inches in the tail.

My turn came for the trip to the Isle of Capri. Command cars took us to the dock to catch the ferry. Danny and her group came back on the ferry we were waiting for, so there was little time to talk.

"Oh, you'll love it," someone exclaimed. "It's so beautiful there!"

"We told them you're coming," said another.

"Nurses there from other hospitals had their new uniforms," said Danny. "They looked gorgeous. I felt like an alley rat but had a good time anyway."

The ferry eased out of the harbor that was crowded with the tangled wreckage of sunken ships. The Isle of Capri appeared as a jagged rock rising out of the sea on the horizon. The trip to the island took two hours.

The ferry stopped at the bottom of the high cliff walls. We climbed steep stairs to the top. Enlisted men in Jeeps met us at the top and took us to the hotel. We were guests of the air force, which used the island as a rest camp.

"Have you ever seen anything so beautiful?" I whispered to Mary, as we crossed the lobby on thick carpets and with crystal chandeliers overhead. I felt like Alice in Wonderland. Everything was white: the walls, the carpet, and the furniture.

Our huge room had high ceilings. A warm breeze through a small opening in the window rippled the curtains. A heavy white brocade spread covered a king-sized bed. We opened the three large windows and marveled at the panoramic view of the deep blue Mediterranean, the harbor, and Naples beyond.

"Avis! Come look at this!" called Mary from the private bathroom. It had white marble fixtures. The towels were the size of bedsheets. We pulled back the spread and found sheets of pure linen! Three white overstuffed chairs were near the window.

"I think I'll just stay in this room for the next five days," I said.

War was far away for the moment.

"It's time for dinner," said Mary. "I wonder if it will be as sumptuous as everything else here."

"I'm sure it'll be because the air force gets nothing but the best."

The dining room was as luxurious as our room. Small tables with white linen tablecloths filled the brightly lit room. Strolling musicians stopped at each table to answer requests. The meal was as memorable as our surroundings. Baskets of hard rolls were on each table. We had steak, green salad, and peas. Our last course was spumoni and coffee. The dining room buzzed with happy chatter and laughter.

"I wish we could take some of this back to the 56th with us," said Mary.

"I met someone who wants to go to the piazza tonight," I said. "He's a friend of Danny's."

We strolled to the piazza located in the center of the island. It was dusk and the air was warm. Natives, along with military personnel, filled the square. The lovely little shops were mostly empty. After stopping at every shop, I found one with stationery and a few pieces of jewelry. My date and I returned to the hotel for a dance with a live orchestra. Everything appeared magical compared to Dragoni.

Morning brought another treat—breakfast in bed. The waiter knocked at the door and came in. He put two bed trays in front of us and opened the napkins with a flourish. We had fresh squeezed orange juice, rolls, coffee, and two eggs, sunny side up.

"What're you doing today?" asked Mary.

"Sam asked me to go to the Blue Grotto with some of our group," I replied. "I hear we shouldn't miss seeing it. What are you doing?"

"I'm going to stay here at the hotel," said Mary.

We descended the steep stairs and met an elderly, wrinkled Italian waiting with a boat that resembled a canoe. We wondered how six more adults could ride in the small craft. Our guide paddled along the base of the tall cliffs until we reached an opening no higher than the boat. We lay down while the old gentleman skillfully guided the boat through the small opening.

Once inside, we sat up, and the sight that greeted us was breathtaking! The huge dome-shaped room and the water were a light shade of azure blue. Everything, including our faces, took on the

Lt. Avis Dagit in new olive-crab uniform

same shade of blue from the reflection of the water. We stayed at the grotto for half an hour. We followed the cliff closely to the foot of the stairs. We again climbed the stairs, dressed for dinner, and were ready for another round of evening parties.

Our leave was over. We packed our meager belongings, descended the stairs once more, and boarded the ferry back to Naples. Naples was gray, battered, and dirty compared to Capri. Fighting did not touch the island. Transportation from the hospital waited for us at the dock. We had a wonderful time on leave but it was good to see familiar faces. I realized where we belonged and why we were in Italy.

The new uniforms arrived a few days after my leave at Capri. Everyone received quantities of clothing. We got dress uniforms, coats, sweaters, purses, long underwear, and kid gloves. The clothing issue included brown- and-white-striped seersucker dresses and pant uniforms for duty. Everything was olive drab or brown. We received two pair of oxfords and two pair of ankle-high shoes. Everyone took the ankle-high shoes to the nearest shoemaker and had four-inch extensions added to the top. We tucked our trousers into the combat boots to keep them clean and dry. I lost twenty pounds after I was measured, but the new clothing fit well.

Despite the bitter fighting, the front made little movement. We evacuated patients daily to a station hospital in Naples. Newly wounded soldiers filled the cots each morning. Our troops bogged down along the Gustav Line, a German fortification across Italy. This fortification protected the Liri Valley and was ninety miles south of Rome.

The wounded, and infantrymen on a few days rest, told unbelievable stories of the hardships they endured on the mountainsides. German troops were well protected on higher peaks and the Allies were in the valley. They easily observed any movement of our troops. We looked to the north and saw a red glow from the guns. The red glow to the south was from Mount Vesuvius. The mountain, dormant for many years, stirred to activity as the result of heavy bombing in the Naples area.

Winter approached and morale was often as gloomy as the weather. We had Thanksgiving church services and about fifty attended.

"We should be thankful for Major Willis' talent at the organ," I said to Lena as we left church. "I heard we're going to have turkey for dinner. I'll be thankful for that, too."

Bill, Paul, and Carl prepared a sumptuous feast for our Thanksgiving dinner. We had turkey, sweet potatoes, mashed dehydrated potatoes, cranberries, and mince pie for dessert.

Mail arrived by the Jeep load after Thanksgiving. Along with the letters and cards came packages packed with goodies. Often the packages arrived in poor condition after the long trip. We ate every crumb. Lena and I invited Jon and Whitey to share our treats.

*Mary Henehan, Lena Grussing, Ellen
Ainsworth, and Avis Dagit dressed for duty*

"I hope none of our officer friends show up while they're in our tent," I said to Lena.

"I'll say it's someone from home," she replied.

We made a feeble effort to decorate the wards and create a little Christmas spirit. Most thought of their own homesickness and misery and did not think of anything else. We had church services and little sound passed the lump in my throat when we sang "Silent Night."

Our Christmas dinner of turkey and all the trimmings was more bountiful than at Thanksgiving. Ellen tried to spread cheer when she gathered a few friends to sing carols over the public address system. Acoustics were bad and everyone was grateful when the system broke down. Most went to bed glad the day was over.

New Year's Day passed with little observation. General Eisenhower predicted the war would end in 1944 and that boosted our morale more than anything else.

The front made a little movement and other evacuation hospitals leap-frogged over us. The volume of patients slowed and by the middle of January there was only a trickle. We assumed that our air force defeated the Luftwaffe because we had not had any air raids the past few weeks. We knew we would move again soon. We received orders on January 19 to close the hospital and report to a staging area at Caivano, near Naples.

"Where do you think we're going now?" I asked Mary.

"I heard we're going to southern France. Someone said there will be an invasion there."

"Sergeant Price said we're going to the States and train for the Pacific," I said.

"Lordy, I hope not. That would be worse than it is here."

"We'd at least get to stop at home," I said, trying to look on the bright side.

Rumors passed through camp hourly the next few days. We knew the colonel had orders for our next assignment when we heard officer's call on January 21.

We assembled at the headquarters tent and Colonel Blesse came before the group.

"We received orders this morning to proceed to a staging area near Caivano at 0800 hours tomorrow. We'll start loading trucks today. Get your equipment ready so we can move out on time."

"Where's Caivano?" someone asked.

"About twenty miles from here, toward Naples," answered Colonel Blesse.

"What's there?" was another question. "The front is farther east and north."

"I can't tell you more now," answered the colonel impatiently. "We'll get further orders when we get to the staging area. Right now the only thing we need to worry about is getting ready to move. Dismissed."

Warming ourselves around a fire made from C-ration boxes

"Probably another one of those hurry up and wait places," said one of the officers.

The colonel's terse announcement puzzled everyone and it left us with more questions than answers.

Mary and I returned to our tent to start packing.

"We might as well burn these C-ration boxes," I said. "We'll be warm one night before we leave here."

"I'll sure miss mine for a dresser, but we can get more at our next stop."

We made a roaring fire of the boxes and the tent was so warm we opened the flap for a breath of cool air.

I went to sleep wondering where the next move would take us.

Chapter X

Fiery Cauldron

It's time to get up," called Mary. It took all my strength to crawl out of the cozy bedroll. The warm fire of the night before burned out and the morning air was heavy with bone-chilling dampness. The date was January 19, 1944.

We finished packing, went to breakfast, and waited for word as to when the convoy would leave.

Two soldiers tapped on the canvas. "Sorry, but we have to strike this tent."

The ground was fairly dry where the tent had been, so I sat on my barracks bag and wrote a letter home. "Don't worry if you don't hear from me for a while," I wrote. "I'm fine, but everything can change quickly here and it isn't easy to write."

We had lunch from our mess kits and waited. Danny and I found a board for a table and played canasta. Word finally came around 1400 hours that the trucks were lining up and ready to move.

We had added supplies and souvenirs at each stop since leaving the United States less than a year earlier. Our 112-vehicle convoy swelled to 130 vehicles. It took two hours for the twenty-three-mile trip to Caivano. The sun was sinking behind the mountains when we reached camp. A blanket of damp, penetrating chill enveloped us.

We sat on canvas cots and ate a meal of warm C rations prepared by an advanced detail of men. The temperature dropped even more as darkness fell. Two ward tents and cots provided quarters for the nurses.

"Let's go to the tent for a cigarette," I said to Danny. "Maybe it'll be warmer than it is out here."

"We'll probably have to go to bed early," said Danny. "We can't see to read. There's only one bulb in the whole tent."

"Can't you imagine what it'll be like if we're here long?" I said. "I can already hear the fussing, swearing, and griping!"

"Yeah, a quart of water a day and no showers won't sweeten any dispositions," said Danny with a chuckle.

I took the cot between Mary and Danny because I was cold and tired. I thought, *If I'm miserable, at least I'll be with my friends.* It was too chilly to take off my clothes, so I went to bed fully dressed. I removed my tightly laced combat boots during the night because my feet were numb.

I awakened when some of the early risers said the bugler had played mess call. We had to get up if we wanted breakfast. I dashed cold water on my face and used a little of the precious liquid to brush my teeth. I went to join others in the chow line and thought, *Maybe we won't be here long.*

"I didn't talk to anyone who knew when we would leave here," I said to Danny. "Did you?"

"I heard a lot of rumors, but nothing official," she said. "We might as well play cards until we find something else to do."

Danny and I, bundled in long, wool-lined trench coats, joined others huddled near by. Rumors were rampant and we listened to all of them. We sought any activity that would break the monotony of waiting. Some of the men started a pickup ball game and we cheered our favorites. Italian men, women, and children gathered along the seven-foot-high rock wall that surrounded the camp. They bartered for cigarettes, candy, and gum with eggs, fruit, and recently concocted wine. They serenaded us several times a day with popular Italian songs and arias from famous operas.

Wave after wave of our heavy bombers, flying north, filled the sky overhead several times each day. Everyone fell silent and watched until they were out of sight. We all knew an airman's peril during daylight raids on German installations. We counted the bombers when they returned and tried to estimate our losses.

We became tired of waiting, no showers, and eating C rations from mess kits. Living in close quarters with forty others left everyone with little personal space. We lifted our spirits by singing and warmed ourselves around a bonfire before we went to bed.

We followed the war in the *Stars and Stripes*. We read on January 22 of an Allied invasion behind enemy lines at Anzio-Nettuno, thirty miles south of Rome. The landing took the Germans by surprise and was successful. They needed hospitals to service the troops on the beachhead and we were ready to go.

We went on alert and waited all day on January 23 for further orders.

"I'd think they'd try to get us to the beachhead as soon as possible," I said to Mary.

"Maybe there isn't much fighting there," she said. "You know the colonel said we took the Germans by surprise."

"Well, if I had my choice, I wouldn't choose to go to a beach in January."

We got up on January 24 and started another day of waiting. It was dark when Colonel Blesse called us together at 1700 hours. "Our orders just came," he began. "We will leave at 1900 hours."

We ate a quick meal of K rations. Everyone made a trip to the water truck for a ration of one quart of water. I donned my helmet, put on the belt with canteen and mess kit, and picked up my musette bag. I was ready to go. We finally left at 2200 hours.

We huddled together to stay warm in the open truck for the twenty-mile trip to the port of Pozzuoli, Naples. The night was pitch dark and the convoy moved slowly over the winding road in blackout conditions. Everyone was sleepy and hungry, but the thought of being aboard a ship soon buoyed our spirits. We would sail the next morning for the eight-hour trip to Anzio.

We jumped from the trucks when we reached the port and waited for orders. It was total blackout, without even a flashlight. Who was in charge? Loaded with our gear, we waited on the dock. Finally a captain called, "Nurses over here."

Ships crowded the harbor. When he led us to an LCI, a chorus of groans went up.

"Not another LCI!" moaned one of the girls.

"I get sick just thinking about it," said another.

"I'll be all right if I can get to sleep before I'm sick," I said to Danny.

The signs were ominous. This wasn't going to be a luxury cruise.

"Nurses' quarters below," shouted a sailor, who directed us toward the ladder to the lower deck.

"This must be a British ship. That wasn't an American sailor," I said to Danny, who was ahead of me.

We had started down the narrow, rusty stairs when Danny turned suddenly and said, "Let me out of here! I saw a rat."

"Sorry, I can't," I said. "There are too many people behind me and this ladder is too narrow for you to get by them."

A rat was a small distraction considering other hardships on the boat.

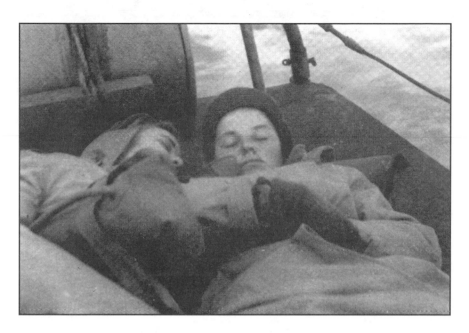

Catching a few winks on deck of LCI on way to Anzio

All nurses were in the same quarters. Bunks were three deep with barely enough room to walk between them. A dim yellow light bulb hung at the foot of the stairs. The choking, stale air was heavy with fumes from the ship's motors, and breathing was difficult.

"I'll take the top bunk this time," I said. The bunk was near the stairs. I thought it would be easier to get topside for a breath of fresh air.

"Where are the blankets?" asked Danny.

"Looks like we don't get any," I said. "And my trench coat is in my bed roll. This slicker won't be a very warm cover. Oh, well; I can stand anything for one night."

I hung my helmet, musette bag, and belt with canteen and mess kit on the end of the bunk. I shifted and squirmed on the canvas bunk and tried to tuck the slicker around me. I wanted to fall asleep before I got sick. When I was getting settled, I heard male voices coming down the stairs.

"The latrine doesn't work down here," explained the British captain to Colonel Blesse, who was following closely behind.

"Don't worry," Colonel Blesse assured him proudly. "My girls will manage just fine if you'll give them a bucket."

My bunk was just a few feet from the offensive bucket. I heard retching and knew some of the nurses were sick. We were still in the harbor when the chill air, odors, and claustrophobia started taking its toll. Those that could not reach the bucket used their helmets for an emesis basin. Someone was at the bucket all night and I got very little sleep. It was a relief when morning came.

"Get up, Danny," I said, shaking her awake. "Let's go on deck for our breakfast. I need air and I want to get out of this smelly hole."

We moved slowly out of the harbor at 0800 hours. Battleships, cruisers, LSTs, and destroyers filled the horizon as far as the eye could see. The protection of the harbor made the sea appear calm and portended little of what lay ahead. We sat on deck and leaned against the cabins to eat breakfast. They also shielded us from the wind that began to rise when we reached open water.

"I'm not going to drink much water because I don't want to use that bucket," I said. "I'll wait until I get on land to brush my teeth."

The K rations took the edge off my hunger.

"I wonder what happened to the rest of our personnel and equipment," I said. "The doctors and nurses are the only ones on this ship."

"We're all on British ships," said Danny, who always had the latest information. Four other ships carried the administrative officers, 315 enlisted men, and equipment.

The winds reached gale force and tossed the small ship like a cork over waves that threatened to capsize us. We hugged closely to the cabin when we stood to stretch and move around. Two ropes around the slippery, wet deck gave little protection from sliding into the angry sea. My face was stiff and taut from the saltwater spray, but the air was fresh and cool. Danny and I spent the day dozing, fighting nausea, and speculating on what lay ahead. There was little activity on board because the sick nurses no longer left their bunks.

It got dark early, and I asked a sailor who came by on his rounds of the deck, "When will we get to Anzio?"

"I don't know, ma'am. This is the worst storm to hit the Mediterranean in recent memory and we haven't made much headway."

The sky was as dark as the swirling sea around us. Around 1800 hours, I said to Danny, "Looks like we'll spend another night on this tub. We might as well go below and try to get some sleep."

I heard moans and groans when I started down the ladder. *If I can get to sleep before I'm sick, I'll be okay,* I thought. I was trying to get to my bunk when a thunderous crash rocked the ship. Had the Germans spotted the convoy?

Mary shouted down the stairs, "The captain said we can transfer to an LST. Better hurry. We can't stay here long."

"I'll go. It's bound to be better than this," I shouted back.

I got back into the slicker and slipped the canteen belt around my waist. I grabbed my musette bag and put on my helmet. I wanted my helmet handy in case we had an air raid. I lost little time scrambling up the ladder to the upper deck. It was pitch dark. Sailors, officers, and nurses crowded the tiny deck. The din of anxious voices mingled with those shouting orders in preparation for the transfer. The momentum of the crowd pushed me to the side of the ship where a much larger ship loomed overhead. The ships crashed together and bobbed up and down on the turbulent sea. How would I scale the impossible height to the deck of the other ship? The sailors on the LST threw a rope to the men on deck. They hurriedly tied it around my waist.

I prayed, "Dear God, give me strength and don't let me fall."

I dared not look down. If I missed a step, the ships crashing together would crush me between them. I knew I would drown if I fell into the angry black sea. I scurried up the Jacob's ladder to the deck of the LST. The brave sailors carried out this dangerous maneuver for twenty-six nurses. Their only source of light was a shielded flashlight.

The sailors helped us over the railing and ushered us into the bright, warm inner cabins. One of the crew brought stewed tomatoes and bread. "I'm sorry we can't offer you more to eat." The warm food tasted like a banquet. We'd had two dry crackers, a small tin of cheese, and two pieces of hard candy in the past twenty-four hours.

The immediate crisis was over and I wondered who else had made the transfer. I saw Mary and Ellen, but where was Danny?

"She decided not to come," said Ellen. "Said she wanted to stay with those that were too sick to transfer." Was I selfish to think of myself? I realized why I enjoyed having Danny for a friend.

"We don't have special quarters for women so you can sleep anywhere you can find a spot," said the captain.

I found a wonderful leather couch in the officer's lounge and slept well despite the rolling and lunging of the ship. The LCT was luxurious. I felt fortunate to escape the dismal conditions on the LCI. A sailor came to the lounge near morning.

"Is this your first trip to Anzio?" I asked.

"No, ma'am. We went in with the first wave during the landing," said the sailor. "This is our first trip with a cargo of dynamite and high-octane gasoline." Hearing this shook my sense of security.

We approached Anzio toward evening. Destroyers, battleships, cargo vessels, and landing craft crowded the harbor. An umbrella of silver barrage balloons, which interfered with low-flying aircraft, floated overhead. The activity in the harbor left little doubt that we had sailed into dangerous waters. Everyone was anxious to land as we gathered on deck with our gear.

The first red alert came when we'd been in the harbor only thirty minutes. Sirens screamed and the call to "man your stations" sounded. Sailors rushed in every direction. We dashed to the inner cabins and huddled in fear with throats so tight that even breathing was difficult. The ship shuddered with repercussions from guns firing at German planes overhead. The sky filled with puffs of black smoke and red tracer bullets from antiaircraft guns on shore. The fierce battle lasted forty minutes and left no doubt that the Luftwaffe was still alive. This was Jerry's way of welcoming us to the beachhead.

Uneasy calm, punctuated with shells exploding nearby, filled the night. Red alerts and German planes overhead arrived at dawn. Allied planes met them and engaged in fierce dog fights over our heads. Bombs screamed and we felt the spray when they fell into the water. Our antiaircraft guns scored a few hits and a German plane spiraled into the water, barely missing our ship. We thought only of protecting ourselves and prayed no bombs would fall on us. The raids continued all day and got steadily worse.

When darkness fell, it was obvious we would spend another night on the ship. I could not fall asleep and wondered if our lives would end on the ship in the Anzio harbor.

The next morning brought more shellings and air raids. Everyone was feeling desperate.

"I'll get us off this ship, if possible," said Colonel Rippy, commander of our unit.

Colonel Rippy was finally able to reach officials on shore. They granted us permission to land after he explained that he had a group of nurses on board. We gathered twice for debarkation and were chased back each time by German planes overhead. It had been thirty-six hours since we'd arrived at Anzio. During that time, we'd survived fourteen air raids and countless shellings. I thanked God I was alive.

Outside of frayed nerves, we escaped unharmed. We went ashore on D-day plus five—January 27, 1944.

After the harrowing experiences aboard ship, everyone longed for the security of being on land again. In peacetime, Anzio-Nettuno was a fashionable seaside resort area, the summer playground of wealthy Romans. We expected to be on the beach a short time before the troops moved inland. The terrain was flat, unlike the mountains near Naples. Little did we realize that our first thirty-six hours ashore would be a foretaste of what lay ahead.

Instead of a hero's welcome, men on shore shouted, "What the hell are women doing here? This place is hot. Take the first vehicle you can and get out of here."

Sailors and soldiers unloaded supplies at a feverish pace. All troops were in full battle dress. Armored tanks, trucks, artillery, and men clogged the road leading from the harbor. An open truck waited to take us to the hospital site. Few civilians were on the streets because they had fled to safety in the surrounding hills. The rumble of guns told us that the front was not far away.

We rushed aboard the truck, but the sirens immediately blasted their warning—German planes overhead. Everyone jumped from the truck and pressed against the last remaining wall of a bombed building. American planes swooped in, guns blazing, and chased the intruders back to their territory.

It was a relief to get away from the harbor. Soldiers gaped at us from their hideouts along the dusty road and shouted, "Women don't belong here! Get out as fast as you can!"

We joined the advanced detail of men and officers at the hospital site about three miles east of the village of Nettuno. The original plan was to set up the hospital in a tuberculosis sanatorium near the beach. After the buildings had received direct bomb hits the two previous nights, officials

First twenty-six nurses on beachhead
Ellen Ainsworth kneeling lower left;
Avis Dagit in front of male officer, back row

changed the plans to make it a hospital because they believed the sanatorium was a military target.

It was comforting to see our men who had come a few days before us.

"How is it here?" I asked.

"It's been hell. Air raids all day and shelling all night. That's the front over there by those trees," said one man. He pointed across the barren landscape to a line of trees about a mile away.

"Better start digging a foxhole," said another.

A few tents set up on a broad expanse of sandy beach marked our location. A makeshift kitchen prepared an evening meal of warm C rations. We set up cots for the rest of the personnel because we expected them momentarily.

Red crosses on a white background marked hospitals. There was a cross on each tent and a much larger one on the ground in the center of the compound. We took some comfort in the fact the red crosses were off limits to combat activity and respected by the enemy. No one wanted a visit from the German air force. The men laid the red crosses to mark the area at daybreak.

Darkness came early and the area was in strict blackout. We were glad to go to bed. I looked forward to a night of sound sleep after our "cruise" from Naples. We had barely settled down when a loud, chilling scream pierced the stillness. It grew louder and louder when it passed overhead. The ground shook when the missile landed with a thunderous thud beyond us.

"My God, what was that?" whispered someone, as if she was afraid the sound of her voice would attract the enemy.

"Sounds like shells to me," I answered, my voice choked with fear.

This happened again and again during the night. I was afraid to go to sleep and lay paralyzed with fear. It was a relief to see the first hint of light after a night with little sleep. We had a better idea where the shells came from when we moved around in the daylight. We saw the harbor, not far away, and knew this was one of the German targets.

"I wonder where the rest of the personnel are," someone said.

"They should be here by now," said another. "We all left Naples together."

"We can't set up the hospital until we get supplies," I whispered to Mary.

Colonel Blesse called us together to calm our nerves and reassure us. "There is nothing to worry about and you won't need to dig foxholes," he said. He pointed to the hills to the south and east. "Those hills are ours and the troops only have to take the ones to the north and we expect to have them by nightfall. The situation is well in hand. You can write to the folks at home and tell them you're on the Anzio Beachhead."

The pep talk did little to soothe our shattered nerves when German planes appeared overhead with American fighter planes in pursuit. The planes dived and swooped with guns blazing. Puffs of black smoke filled the sky and the rat-a-tat-tat of antiaircraft guns sent up a deafening roar.

"Get him! Get him!" we shouted, even though the gunners could not hear us.

We saw an American plane spiral downward, leaving a trail of smoke. "Oh! That Jerry got our plane!" we cried in anguish. The pilot ejected and slowly drifted to earth. We ducked the dirt and flames that shot skyward when the plane plummeted to earth two hundred yards away. A German plane fell across the road from where we were standing at about the same time. The other German planes disappeared into the morning sunshine.

"I should write letters home," I said to Mary while we walked slowly back to our tent. "I'm not going to tell the folks where I am, though. It'll only cause them to worry."

My family found out soon when word passed quickly that American nurses were on the beachhead. Foreign correspondents came searching for anyone from their home territory for a story to send home.

Ellen came to our tent and said, "Avis, there is a reporter looking for you."

I went to the headquarters and recognized Gordon Gammack from the Des Moines *Register*. I had been on duty at Iowa Methodist Hospital when his daughter had been born two years earlier.

We talked of home and Iowa, which seemed so far away.

"How do you feel about being in a place as dangerous as this?" he asked.

"If the boys can take it, we can," I said. "They're in greater danger." He relayed the story home along with my picture. My family suffered great anguish when the war went badly for us in the days ahead.

Even though Colonel Blesse told us foxholes were unnecessary, many of the officers and men started to dig anyway. It was easy to dig in the sandy beach. The water table was high and the holes quickly filled with water. However, many dug holes in a drainage ditch that bordered the camp and they remained dry. The bank of the ditch soon resembled a prairie dog village. Nurses could not find the time or did not have enough strength to dig a hole. We always wore a steel helmet. Those without one received a twenty-five dollar fine. The order was enforced easily.

Air raids continued for the next two days. The big railroad gun that the Germans pulled from a tunnel in the mountains shelled all night. We learned that the gun fired one-quarter-ton missiles that made a bone-chilling whistle when they traveled overhead. We soon referred to it as the "Anzio Express." The gun terrorized us and caused much loss of life and valuable equipment during the seventy-six days we were on the beachhead.

All of our personnel and most of the equipment arrived by February 28 with stories of a hazardous trip from Pozzuoli. I was especially happy to see Danny. "What happened on the ship after I left?" I asked.

"We got to Anzio, but the sea was too rough to dock," she said. "We returned to Pozzuoli and sailed again last night. I'm happy to be on land again after our rough ride."

I saw Jon Peters later and asked about his experience. "Our ship broke in two during the storm when we were a short distance from Pozzuoli. We drifted back to the harbor and transferred to another ship."

Men from all five of the ships had a story to tell. The motor went dead on one ship and it bobbed on the sea several hours. After some repairs, it limped back to harbor. Another ran short of fuel and could not reach Anzio. One with supplies and eleven men was on the trip four days at the mercy of the sea. Everyone had undergone many air raids and shellings. We felt fortunate to arrive safely despite our harrowing experiences. Now that all the hospital personnel were together again, we were ready to set up the hospital and care for battle casualties.

Chapter XI

Sea of Wounded

Everyone pitched in and set up cots and prepared the operating room, laboratory, pharmacy, x-ray, and other needed services. We resterilized all surgical supplies because seawater had contaminated them. Fighting was fierce and there was a critical need for hospitals.

Setting up the hospital was more difficult than expected because many of our supplies were still on the docks awaiting transportation to the hospital site. The army needed every truck to haul ammunition, equipment, and supplies to the front. The uneasy quiet of D-Day had vanished long ago. Our men fought desperately to keep the Germans from pushing us into the sea.

Men pitched two-person tents for our permanent quarters. Every minute was precious, so they did not take time to set up cots. Bedrolls, barracks bags, musette bags, and personal supplies were thrown hastily inside the tent. We did not have electricity and the entire beachhead was under strict blackout conditions. Darkness settled quickly after sunset and I needed to find two cots under the pile of gear before I went to sleep: one for myself and one for Mary when she could be spared for a few minutes' rest from the grueling duty in the operating room.

The Germans employed another weapon against us—the glider bomb. A motorless ship, with a bomb attached, came in noiselessly and dropped its missile. One fell short during a raid on the harbor the evening of January 29 and missed the hospital by less than 150 yards. It sent a geyser of mud and flames skyward and left a twenty-five-by-sixty-foot crater.

Later the same evening, it was dark when I reached the tent Mary and I shared. I lifted the flap to enter when a deafening explosion shook the ground. Pain shot through both ears. A glider bomb had struck an ammunition ship, exploding in a brilliant fire that silhouetted other ships in the harbor. More blasts rocked the ship, sending black balls of smoke into the sky. Raging fire on the burning ship reflected on the canopy of silver barrage balloons that floated over the harbor and lit the entire skyline. Troops arrived on the beachhead as quickly as the army and navy could send them, but I felt alone. What was going to happen to us? We were cut off from the rest of the world and depended upon the shipping lanes for our supplies. I thought about the men on the damaged ships, a senseless loss of life.

Death, doom, and disaster surrounded us. I wanted to run, but there was no place to go. My throat was tight and my heart pounded until I thought it would burst my chest. Fear paralyzed me for a few minutes. I went inside the tent. The air was damp and chilly as soon as the sun set, so I did not take off my woolen shirt and trousers. I found a cot and fell upon it, burying my head under my arms. The scream of the Anzio Express overhead added to the noise of battle around me. Despite the shock of the explosion, I finally fell asleep. Everyone reported for duty the next morning.

We received the first casualties at noon on January 30. Others quickly followed, and by evening the wounded filled all surgical wards. Medical wards, the dental clinic, and supply tents became receiving wards. A steady flow of ambulances brought wounded to the hospital all day and all night.

An overwhelming number of casualties taxed our resources to the limit. We started working in the morning and everyone stayed on duty for the night.

Wounded sprawled everywhere in all the ward tents. Seeing so many men with bloody, mangled bodies horrified me. I was reminded of the similar scene in *Gone with the Wind*. I had barely enough room to walk between the rows of litters in the dimly lit tent. Despite the numbers, it was eerily quiet. No one complained or cried out. The men were in shock from the brutal fighting. We heard the guns raging a short distance away. I examined each man's wounds and wanted to cry when they thanked me for the kindness. Most quietly lit a cigarette or helped those unable to help themselves. I asked each man if he needed anything. A few with severe wounds asked only to be put to sleep.

We submitted a list of patients needing immediate surgical care. We sent those with sucking chest wounds, abdominal cases, traumatic amputations, or uncontrolled bleeding to surgery first. Despite surgery working as painstakingly and quickly as they could, we evacuated the less seriously wounded by boat to Naples for further care.

Our hospital was the first one on the beachhead. A shortage of supplies added to the burden of caring for the huge number of wounded. We ran out of intravenous fluids and called upon the men in the Sixth Corps headquarters and Seabees to replenish our blood bank.

Captain Meadors came to the ward about 0400 hours and said, "Lieutenant Dagit, it looks like everything is under control here. Would you go to Pre-op Number 1 for a while? They desperately need help."

"Most of the men are sleeping," I said. "I've reported the most seriously wounded to Captain Martin."

"They need someone to mix plasma. When you're fifty units ahead, you can come back here."

Pre-op #1 held the most critical cases who would be going to surgery first. I walked through the inky blackness, avoiding tripping over tent poles, toward #1. I hadn't eaten in twenty-four hours, but I wasn't thinking of food. My legs were heavy and the sight of the endless number of wounded seared my mind. I was neither emotionally nor physically prepared for the shock and horror that greeted me.

I opened the tent flap and a scream stuck in my throat. The smell of blood and flesh hit me. I saw litter after litter filled with men wounded beyond description. Blood-soaked bandages covered stumps of missing limbs. Some men had their faces shot away. Others had suffered abdominal wounds and attendants had to keep the bandages moist until they went to surgery. Blood-soaked, mud-caked uniforms were cut away to reveal gaping wounds in arms, legs, and torso. Bottles of plasma, dripping into every man, lined the ceiling of the tent. We prepared this life-saving liquid by mixing the contents of two vacuum bottles. One bottle held saline and the other dried blood-plasma cells.

I went to the makeshift table and quickly mixed plasma and prayed I could keep up with the demand. My hunger and fatigue were not important considering the critical situation in the pre-op tent.

I glanced up and saw Capt. Madge Teague, an anesthetist, enter the ward. She went from litter to litter and examined each soldier's wounds. She came to a litter where a young, blond soldier lay under the light of a bare bulb. Beads of perspiration stood on his forehead. His face, including his lips, was deathly white. One leg, still in a combat boot, twisted at a crazy angle. Bandages covered a wound on his chest. She crouched down and gently removed the bandage. A five inch square of flesh was gone and his ribs glistened through the gaping wound. Tears streamed down my cheeks, making it difficult to continue mixing the plasma. My fifteen-year-old brother at home looked so much like this young soldier.

"When will I go to surgery?" asked the soldier weakly. "Will I be all right?"

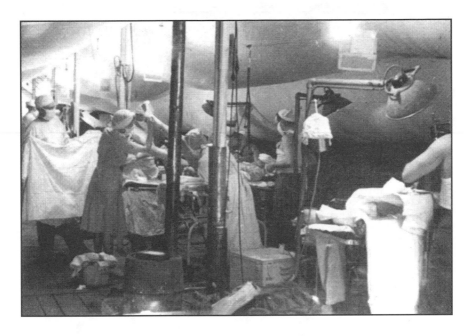

Operating room at Anzio

"We'll get to you very soon," said Captain Berg. She laid her hand tenderly on the soldier's forehead. I never doubted she cared for every patient with the same compassion.

When morning came, I reported to Captain Meadors, who was making rounds of the wards. Her small shoulders sagged under the responsibility of staffing the hospital. She asked, in a weary voice, "Could you stay on duty another twelve hours? I'm sorry because I know you need sleep, but I don't have anyone to relieve you."

"Could I have a cup of coffee first, and where do you want me to go?"

"You can go back to your own ward and I promise I won't ask you to work another shift."

I went to the mess hall and revived myself emotionally and physically with coffee and a bowl of oatmeal. The images of the wounded in Pre-op #1 swam in my mind.

The patients I saw twelve hours earlier were gone and the tent was full of newly wounded.

One soldier said, "I'd rather be at the front than in here. We have a fox-hole there."

"So would I," chimed in several others.

We made a list of patients for evacuation.

"I don't want to ride down that road to the harbor," said a soldier with shrapnel wounds in his legs. "I'd like to see Naples, but I can wait."

"Yeah, those krauts in the hills watch every move we make."

"They shoot at everything that moves on the road, even the meat wagons," said another. The soldiers named the road "Purple Heart Alley" because it was a favorite target for shelling.

In our first thirty-six hours, the hospital admitted 1,129 battle casualties. The 750-bed hospital expanded to 1,200 by adding more tents.

The day passed quickly and again it was dark and the shift was over. Despite being on duty for thirty-six hours, I felt quite well physically. I again went to bed fully clothed and slept despite two air raids and the shells, too numerous to count, that screamed overhead.

More hospitals arrived on the beachhead, among them the 93rd Evac, the 33rd Field Hospital, and the 95th Evac. This relieved some of the load on our facilities. We had been friends with the 95th Evac ever since we sailed to North Africa together on the Mariposa in April of 1943. I looked forward to seeing Gertrude Mark again, a friend from our days at Iowa Methodist Hospital in Des Moines. We would talk about home, but that could wait until the situation on the beachhead stabilized.

The Germans shelled the 33rd Field Hospital just after they arrived. Hoping the enemy could identify us more clearly, officials grouped all hospitals together. The 56th was the hub and Colonel Blesse was commander of the medical facilities. The compound was between the harbor and the Alban Hills behind us occupied by the Germans. It soon became known as

"Hell's Half Acre" because it was one of the most feared places on the beachhead.

Ammunition dumps, motor vehicle pools, fuel dumps, and artillery surrounded the hospital compound. The navy trained their guns on the German lines and the Germans shelled the harbor. Shells and bombs fell short a few times and landed in the hospital, but they did not injure anyone. Most managed to carry on without a great deal of panic and fear despite shattered nerves and sleepless nights. Less seriously wounded patients continued to plead for a discharge to the front because they felt safer in their foxholes there.

It was difficult to differentiate between day and night because it was dark when we went on duty and dark when our shift was over. We didn't think about working twelve hours and then having twelve off because the flow of patients never let up. How long would this go on? I walked slowly to my tent after a shift of night duty. I could not erase the image of every cot filled with newly wounded men. The odor of fresh blood and wet plaster hung over the entire ward. These were the lucky ones. How many had died?

A man from the rangers had his right arm shattered and many pieces of shrapnel still in his body. He said, "The shell that hit me blew my buddy away. I was lucky. That shell didn't have my name on it." Our survival depended upon the luck of the draw. I didn't want to think about it. Nothing could prepare me for the next few days.

The Evacuation Department came through each morning to carry the wounded to waiting ambulances for the trip to Naples for further care. They left everything except their billfolds, which they clutched almost reverently to their chests. Money had no value here, but the pictures inside were their link with home in this insane war. I swallowed hard and fought back the tears. My heart ached for every one of them.

On one of the first mornings, after a night of duty, I went outside for a breath of fresh air before I found my tent for some much-needed sleep.

It was quiet and I tried to imagine what it had been like on the beautiful beach before the war tore everything apart. I again thought about the 95th Evac in the same area and wanted to look for Gertrude. Maybe there would be time to find her before I went on duty again.

Despite exhaustion, I preferred to be on the wards, because my tent was dark and lonely, not a retreat from the agony and suffering around me. I longed for a bath, but there was no way to heat the water. I hated to be without my helmet handy and the cold water would make it hard to fall asleep. I forgot about bathing, crawled into the sleeping bag, and soon fell into deep, exhausted sleep.

I had been asleep for several hours when I heard planes overhead and gunfire close by—or was I dreaming? I slid deeper into the sleeping bag and covered my head. I shifted and turned, trying to block out the noise.

Mary burst into the tent. "Thank God, Avis! You're all right!"

"What was all that noise? I could hardly sleep."

"Oh, I'm so glad you're all right," cried Mary, her words spilling out hysterically. "It's so terrible—the 95th was bombed. We don't know how many are killed. We're working on the wounded and surgery is swamped."

"Was anyone we know killed?" I asked, afraid to hear her answer.

"The chief nurse and a Red Cross worker were killed instantly. Most of the patients in the post-op ward were killed. Your friend, Gertrude, is critically wounded. The doctors don't think she'll survive. She's in surgery now."

My head swam with despair and grief. I heard excited, anxious voices in the distance and hoped I'd hear that this horrible massacre was not true.

"Do you have to go back on duty?" I asked pleadingly.

"I could get away only for a minute to see if you were okay," said Mary, and I heard her running as soon as she got outside the tent.

I thought about the chief nurse who was from Ft. Dodge, a neighboring town in Iowa. Sweet, gentle Gertrude was helpful and kind when I was a freshman in nurses' training. I looked to her for guidance even in the war. She survived the bombing at Salerno and I prayed for her at Anzio.

I lay on my cot for an hour and stared at the top of the dark tent. I fought choking emotions of grief, fright, and anger. I was angry at Hitler, the Germans, and the war that put us here. My heart ached and it was hard to breathe. I realized any breath could be my last.

I learned later that the carnage happened when German planes flew over the beachhead. Allied planes were in hot pursuit. Jerry, trying to lighten his load and escape, jettisoned his anti-personnel bombs. The bombs landed on the hospital, killing twenty-six and wounding sixty-eight. The bombs killed or wounded everyone in the pre-op ward, including many already wounded while fighting on the front. The Allies shot down the plane when it tried to get away. This tragedy was hard on our morale. The bombing badly crippled the hospital, and they left the beachhead. The 15th Evac replaced the 95th. I was sleeping about 150 yards from where the bombs fell. This happened on February 7, 1944.

A tap, tap on the tent brought me to my feet. It was Jon.

"I just wanted to see if you're all right," said Jon.

"How is Gertrude Morrow?" I asked anxiously.

"She died."

I wanted to cry, but the hurt was so deep, tears would not come. I was numb and did not want to believe what I heard.

"Couldn't they do anything to save her?" I cried.

"The bomb blew her leg off at the hip" said Jon. "She also lost her kidneys. Her life wouldn't have been worth living." I found little comfort in his words.

"There isn't any place that's safe here, is there?" I asked despairingly. "What are we going to do? The men wounded at the front are killed in the hospital."

"First, I think you'd better dig a foxhole," said Jon. "I'd help you, but I can't get away because we're so busy in receiving."

"Maybe I could dig a hole inside the tent if there's enough room," I said. "Canvas isn't much protection, but I hate to be outside alone."

"Why don't you dig half outside and put your head and upper body inside?"

That sounded reasonable to me because I was afraid of getting hit in the head more than anything.

"I'm working a few hours tonight and will be working tomorrow. Could you bring a litter and I'll put it inside the hole so I can sleep there? Nighttime is the worst because I might not wake up during an air raid."

When I got off duty the next evening, the litter Jon had promised was propped against the tent. I found an empty plasma can on the ward to use for a shovel. I lit a candle and sat on the cold, wet ground to dig. I shook from the cold, the two red alerts, and the whistle of shells overhead. Despite digging furiously, progress was slow because the wet sand stuck in the can. I abandoned the can and dug with my bare hands, packing each handful around the excavation. The hole was large enough for the litter when I quit at midnight. I'd put in the refinements the next evening. After shedding my damp clothes, I went to bed feeling more physically secure than I had in several days.

As soon as I opened my eyes the next morning, I looked at the hole to see what else needed to be done. To my dismay, the hole was full of water and the litter floated at ground level. I did not have time to agonize over my misfortune because it was time for breakfast and another day on the wards.

We did not spend much time in the mess hall because mealtime was a favorite time for Jerry to pay us a visit. Tables—planks over sawhorses— were outside the tent. During one daylight shelling of the hospital area, pots and pans flew skyward when shells hit the kitchen. Fortunately, they did

Lt. Loretta Bass

not hurt anyone, but they did shorten mealtime. We no longer concerned ourselves about adding a few pounds. The stress of work, sleepless nights, bombing, and shelling made a very effective weight-loss program.

After trying to dig a foxhole, I needed to devise an alternate plan. I wanted to go to bed and sleep when I got off duty. Maybe we'd be lucky and not have any air raids. I put on my helmet before going to bed to be on the safe side. Sleeping in the steel helmet gave me a stiff neck, but I would recover quickly.

Before I could find a comfortable spot, the red alert sounded and I heard the drone of planes overhead. I looked outside. Flares, dropped from German planes, floated downward, lighting the area with a blinding greenish-white light. Bombs whistled and crashed into the earth nearby with an explosive thud. The antiaircraft guns sent up a deafening roar and I prayed for the men manning the guns. I crawled under my cot and curled up in a ball. Shaking from terror and the dank, cold ground, I prayed, "Please God, don't let any bombs touch me. If I'm wounded, don't let it be my head." My life marched in front of me. How would word that I was killed or wounded affect my family? Who would find me? Would I ever see home again, and in what condition? The all clear sounded, and I climbed back on the cot and slept fitfully until morning.

After another night of raids, officials decided that the nurses off duty needed an air-raid shelter. Most of us did not have foxholes. A contingent of enlisted men worked into the night digging a hole a few feet below ground. They covered the excavation with four inch posts and a layer of sand.

I saw Ellen at breakfast the next morning and said, "Aren't you glad we have a place to go during a raid?"

"I'm not going to use it," she said. "Everyone will be killed if a bomb hit that shelter. I'll take my chances elsewhere."

"It'll protect us from shrapnel from antipersonnel bombs," I said. "That's Jerry's favorite weapon against us."

I always ran for the shelter during a raid when I was off duty. Ellen told a friend later, "I should go to the shelter to be with Avis because the raids scare her so much."

The Germans shelled our hospital, along with the 33rd Field Hospital, on February 10. The shells killed two nurses and one enlisted man at the 33rd. Our men put out the fire in their generator and carried the wounded to our hospital. The administration sent a detailed map of the hospital area to the German lines. Medical personnel are unarmed and the Geneva Convention rules of war prohibit enemy activity against medical facilities.

No one escaped the feeling of desperation that hung over the beachhead. The Germans had a massive troop buildup ready to launch a counterattack against our infantry. Germans boasted they would make Anzio another Dunkirk. The BBC reported, "President Roosevelt is conferring with high military officials about the gravity of the situation at Anzio." We would be forced to surrender or be evacuated to ships waiting in the harbor if our forces did not hold. Officials made plans to evacuate the nurses and later dropped them. They determined that our presence was a morale factor for the wounded. The Germans harassed us further by dropping propaganda leaflets over the beachhead telling us our situation was hopeless. "Axis Sally," the sultry voiced German propagandist, played the latest American music on the radio. She tormented us with stories of life in the United States. Daily invitations were issued: "Nurses come on over. We have many handsome German officers who will take good care of you." These broadcasts angered and amused us. Meanwhile, the news from the Cassino front was discouraging because the Allies were fighting for their lives there, too.

Conditions on the beachhead grew worse each day. The Germans sent the Anzio Express with its quarter-tons shells over our heads with increasing regularity. The enemy detected every move we made from their observation posts in the hills. Everything that moved was a target.

The men partially buried ambulances in the sand to protect their motors from incoming shells. Officers and men with foxholes dug deeper. Shelling came day and night without warning. Air raids came most often at night. Everyone became expert at distinguishing the familiar sound of German planes before the red alert sounded. Before a raid started, my heart pounded and my throat was dry and it was hard to swallow. I wanted to cry out in anguish for everyone on the beachhead, but I hadn't seen the worst yet.

The Germans unleashed their heaviest raid after dark on February 12. I was outside my tent when the red alert sounded. The foreboding tone of the warning left no doubt we should seek shelter. I ran to the air-raid shelter and was just inside when planes dropped flares over the hospital. They lighted the whole area brighter than day. Planes made pass after pass over the hospital, unleashing a deadly load of antipersonnel bombs. Jagged fragments of metal tore into the flesh of anyone near the explosions.

Bombs screamed earthward and landed with a thud. Above the chaos and bedlam, someone shouted, "They're falling on the nurses' tents!"

A soldier ran to the air-raid shelter shouting hysterically, "Is there a doctor in there? We need a doctor!" Before anyone could answer, he said, "Ellen's been hit!"

Ignoring the falling bombs, two soldiers ran out, found a litter, and carried Ellen to the pre-op ward. No one knew the extent of her wounds. I ran toward the pre-op tent when the all clear sounded an hour and a half later. I met a soldier who had just seen her.

"How is she? Is she badly hurt?" My questions tumbled out faster than he could answer them.

"A piece of shrapnel about the size of a quarter pierced her chest. She has a sucking chest wound." When he saw my anxiety, he said, "It's serious, but I think she'll make it."

"Is she conscious? When can I see her?"

"Not right now because they're getting her ready for surgery. She's wide awake and I heard her tell Captain Young her blood pressure was 130/80."

I walked back to the dark tent and fell on my cot knowing there would be little sleep.

"When, O God, is this madness going to stop?" I prayed.

Bomb fragments riddled my tent, which was about six feet from Ellen's. I found a jagged hole in my metal sewing box that was deep inside my barracks bag. We learned later that the Germans flew about two hundred planes in the raid. The Luftwaffe was still alive.

I met Major Meadors on my way to the mess hall the next morning. "How's Ellen?" I asked anxiously.

"She's a pretty sick girl," she said. "I'm going to have you take care of her during the day. I know this will be hard because you're close friends. I'll have Danny Cleaver take care of her at night until she's better."

The wound in Ellen's chest appeared small. The white hot metal passed through the lung into her abdomen and internal injuries were massive. Stomach contents spread throughout her lungs and abdomen, which made her condition grave. We did not discount her indomitable spirit and prayed for her recovery.

In a regular hospital bed, Ellen was on a surgical ward, screened from other patients. A nasogastric tube was in her nostril and intravenous fluids dripped into her arm. I choked back tears when I saw her. She detected my alarm when I approached her bed.

"Don't worry, Avis," she said. "I'm tougher than anything Jerry can throw at us."

"I know you are," I assured her.

She was alert, her color good. That lifted my spirits.

"Was anyone else hurt?" asked Ellen. As always, she was thinking of others.

"No, you're the only one."

"Oh, thank God," she whispered, closing her eyes.

The noise of battle raged in the distance. I held her hand while she dozed and she squeezed my hand tightly when the noise of an exploding shell was close. I prayed God would give me strength to do everything possible for Ellen. Before we had come to Anzio, battle casualties were strangers fighting on the front lines. Now they were close friends. I also came to the choking realization any one of us could be next.

I was glad to see Danny when my shift was over. Her sunny disposition always lifted my spirits. I needed friends now more than ever. It was comforting that Mary was on day duty now and we could spend the evening together. She told of the exhausting duty in the operating room. Her experience and maturity were invaluable. We read to each other the few pieces of mail that arrived, reassured that those at home had not forgotten us.

Front-line casualties told of a massive German troop buildup and possible counterattack. Air raids and shellings increased in number and intensity, but the troops believed the line would hold. The Germans bombed and shelled the hospital three times in the next two days. The gloom and desperation that hung over the beachhead spared no one.

Ellen lost ground each day. She was aroused only when the percussion of a shell was near or the red alert sounded. I believed much of her lethargy was due to heavy narcotics we gave her regularly. Her abdomen was distended and we gave her oxygen through a mask. She remained so mentally alert that I could not dismiss her fighting spirit. I refused to think she would not recover.

We attached the chain with her dog tags, rabbit's foot, four-leaf clover, lucky-seven dice, and St. Christopher medal to her medical record. Captain Sloan, the ward officer, and I were at the desk when he picked up the chain loaded with charms. He said, "She might as well throw this away." I then realized how grave her condition had become.

On February 16, her breathing was shallow and her pale skin ashen. I tried to moisten her parched lips. She waved me away weakly. I could see her life slipping away. At 1000 she reached to remove the oxygen mask.

"Ellen, we'd better leave the mask on," I whispered. She rolled her eyes back and took her last breath.

I was momentarily frozen with shock. I ran to summon Captain Sloan.

"Come quick! She's gone!" I cried hysterically.

We rushed to the bedside but could not revive her. Captain Sloan put his arm around my shoulders and said, "I'm sorry. I know you were good friends. She never had a chance."

Shocked and numb, I couldn't comprehend what had happened. Tears did not come. "You'd better lie down on that empty cot," said Captain Sloan pointing across the tent. "I'll call Captain Meadors."

I lay on the cot for a few minutes. Why couldn't I cry when it hurt so much? I wanted to tell Mary and Danny what had happened. Before I could gather strength, an announcement blared on the public address. "Funeral services for Lieutenant Ainsworth will be at 1430 hours."

Captain Meadors dressed Ellen in the new uniform she'd never worn. Her body, wrapped in two new army blankets, was placed in an ambulance. She was the first fatality among our personnel. A shocked and demoralized group gathered in front of the ambulance. The chaplain offered prayers and a few words of comfort. While the bugler played taps, the sky overhead filled with bombers on their way to bomb German lines. We watched the planes unload over the front and clouds of dust float skyward. The ambulance pulled slowly away for the trip to the cemetery. Then I started to cry.

Captain Meadors came to Mary and me after the service and asked, "Would you gather her personal items, since you were her best friends? We'll send them to her parents." We put her watch, rings, pictures, and fountain pen in a cloth bag and took it to Captain Meadors.

"You can take the rest of the day off," said Captain Meadors. "You'll report to Ward Six in the morning."

The dark tent was more lonely than ever. Ellen loved to sing and her beautiful voice was stilled forever. Why hadn't I insisted she go to the air-raid shelter with me? I thought about her parents' grief when they heard that their "baby" was killed in the war. In despair, I was reliving the past few days when I heard a tap on the tent. It was Jon.

"I thought you might like someone to talk with and perhaps you could use a drink," said Jon. He mixed a cocktail of grapefruit juice and medical alcohol nicknamed "moose milk."

"The Germans started their big counteroffensive at 0530 this morning and casualties are pouring into receiving," said Jon. "The line is pretty thin in places, but most of the men think it will hold."

"What'll we do if it doesn't?"

"I'm sure the officials have a plan. The Germans might take us prisoners, or we might go to boats in the harbor if there's enough time," said Jon. Neither plan relieved my anxiety.

We talked of the day's events and speculated about what to expect next. I was emotionally and physically exhausted. The wards were full of wounded and I needed sleep before going on duty.

"I'll see you tomorrow," said Jon as he was leaving.

While shells from the Anzio Express screamed overhead, I went to bed and prayed I would see another day.

Chapter XII

Sleepless Nights

It was quiet. The shelling had stopped when I awoke the next morning. Had both sides become so exhausted they could no longer wage battle? Daylight was breaking as I made my way across the soft, wet sand toward Ward #6. Tents huddled close together like a group of friends trying to protect each other. I groped in the semidarkness, fearing I would trip over tent poles and ropes. My stomach was in knots from hunger and anxiety about what I would find on the ward. Ward #6 had some of the most critically wounded in the hospital.

I opened the tent flap to enter. Three bare bulbs barely lit the long ward tent. Newly wounded filled all thirty-six cots. The distinctive, sweet smell of brain tissue, which I recalled from days in surgery, hung heavy in the air. The stench of blood mingled with oily emissions from the electric motor on a suction machine. Propped in a sitting position, two soldiers shared the machine to clear secretions from their tracheotomies. Many of the patients suffered wounds of the head and neck. Some had much of their face missing and others had abdominal wounds. A young soldier with a heavily bandaged head cried for his mother. Two with head injuries thought they were still on the battlefield fighting the Germans and cursed softly. Others lay quiet, making only the guttural sounds of the dying. It was clear that many would not have lived to reach the hospital if we had not been close to the front.

"It's been a terrible night," said the night nurse. "We tried to put the most critical near the desk."

"I'll check everyone," I said. "The ward is full so we won't get any new patients."

I walked through the ward, checking each patient's wounds. I stopped at the cot of a soldier with a boyish face, his head swathed in bandages. His face was ghostly white, including his lips. I felt his forehead and it was cool and damp. I could hardly find a pulse and knew his condition was critical. I dashed to the desk to summon the ward officer.

"Hurry to bed number 20!" I cried. I whirled around to hasten to his bedside, nearly bumping into the critically wounded soldier who stood closely behind me.

"Oh, you must not get up," I said in an anguished voice. "If you need something, we'll bring it to you."

I led him back to the cot and gently helped him lie down. He gave me a fixed stare, gasped, and took his last breath. The image of the dying soldier stayed in my mind for many days. I did not dare break down. Critically wounded men surrounded me and I wanted to be strong for their sake.

We spent the day making each patient as physically comfortable as possible. We started intravenous fluids, fed patients, and gave medication for pain. We gave penicillin, available in small amounts for selected patients, every four hours by injection. We did not have most patients long enough for their wounds to become infected. There was, however, the threat of gas gangrene, the most dreaded and deadly of all complications. Gas gangrene, caused by an aerobic bacillus, forms spores and moves rapidly through the tissues giving off a lethal toxin. The bacillus is found in intestines, soiled clothing, and dressings. Barnyards commonly harbored the bacillus. Farms surrounded the beachhead and soldiers sought shelter in the buildings and used them for outposts. We cared for captured German wounded and they appeared more susceptible to the infection than Americans. We speculated it could be due to their physical condition or diet.

A boyish looking German soldier came to the hospital with leg wounds. The sickish, putrid odor of his wounds indicated the unmistakable presence of gas gangrene. Gas gangrene, spread through open wounds, is very contagious. Everyone moved swiftly so other patients would not become infected. Litter bearers came and rushed the soldier through the dark toward the isolation tent.

"Nein! Nein!" shouted the boy hysterically. He fought to get off the litter when they approached the isolation tent.

"We'd better find someone who speaks German to explain this," said one of the litter bearers.

"I'll get Lieutenant Freed. She speaks German," said the other, and ran to the tent next door. He returned shortly with Lt. Nancy Freed.

Nancy spoke softly and held the young man's hand while she explained why were moving him to the other tent. She learned during the conversation that he had spotted a shovel by the tent door and thought we were going to bury him alive. German propaganda indoctrinated their soldiers into believing that the Americans buried enemy wounded alive instead of treating their wounds. Unfortunately, we could not save him and everyone regretted the young soldier's anguish. The German wounded touched us as deeply as those from England, Ireland, Scotland, or any other country.

Air raids and shellings continued at least four a day through February. As the days wore on, everyone grew edgy from lack of sleep. It was cold and rainy for several days at a time, which added to the misery. Gusts of wind swirled sand in our faces and around the tents. Many coped by drinking heavily. The pharmacy dispensed gallons of medical alcohol and the mess provided grapefruit juice for cocktails. Others, exhausted from the constant lack of sound sleep, did not need a sedative. Danny and I attended church at every opportunity and took comfort in the hymns played by Captain Willis. We fervently prayed to the Almighty for protection.

"I should write to the folks before I go on duty tonight," I said to Danny when we were at supper. "I'm sure they're worried." Mail was irregular and Mother wrote that they had not heard from me in some time.

I went to my tent and tried to write, but I could only stare at the paper. I couldn't write about how it was on the beachhead. How could I tell them what an air raid was like? Or how it affected me to see an endless number of wounded and never enough time to care for them properly? Above all, I didn't want them to know how terrified I was during an air raid or shelling. I took my paper thinking I would try again during the night.

The patients were sleeping. Like before, I stared at the paper and couldn't write.

"Where's the *Stars and Stripes*?" I asked the ward attendant. "I'm going to send Ernie Pyle's column home because he tells what it's like here better than I can."

Ernie Pyle wrote, "Anybody around Anzio two days who hasn't had a shell hit within 100 yards of him is just bragging." I thought, *If I'm killed or wounded, the shock won't be as great if they know what it's like here.*

Capt. Whitey Lucas, the commanding general of all beachhead forces, came on February 21 to award citations. The first award was the Silver Star, the nation's second highest combat award, to Capt. Mary Roberts. She was the operating room supervisor and the first woman to receive the honor. The citation cited Mary for bravery and supervision in the operating room during heavy shelling and bombing. Mary, along with two nurses from other hospitals, met under the flagpole to receive their medals. They left their duties only long enough to receive their awards, and there were no witnesses to the ceremony.

We were emotionally and physically exhausted when we got off duty and it helped to gather in groups and talk. There was always someone who buoyed others with their sense of humor.

Nancy, a nurse from Louisiana, drawled, "We aren't going to get out of this place alive."

"If we get hepatitis," said another, "we'd be sent back to Naples. There have been several cases in the hospital."

Nancy jumped up, "I'm going to my tent and pray I get hepatitis."

God answered her prayers. She became violently ill a few days later with hepatitis. Danny was also stricken and she and Nancy left the hospital. I worried about their ride down "Purple Heart Alley" in the ambulance that took them to the dock. I felt a deep loneliness for both of them but thought they might have a better chance of living through the war. Much later, they told me that hepatitis was harder to endure than shells and bombs at Anzio.

Casualties continued at the same rate all through March. Heavy artillery fire was directed toward the lines on both sides, but the front made little movement. Support units that were normally in a relatively safe position suffered casualties at nearly the same rate as front-line troops. Patients with minor wounds concealed them rather than come to the hospital. They preferred to stay at the front where they had foxholes. Hell's Half Acre was among the most feared places on the beachhead.

Air raids and shellings occurred daily. We waited for news that forces at Cassino had broken through enemy lines in the Liri Valley. Our only hope of escape from the beachhead depended on these forces rescuing us. Axis Sally gave daily news broadcasts. It was clear that the Germans watched every move we made from their vantage points in the surrounding hills. Enemy air raids were no longer restricted to nighttime hours. After each Allied raid on enemy lines, we expected a retaliation of hit and run raids on us. The deadly accurate eighty-eight-millimeter artillery gun joined the Anzio Express in the arsenal directed toward us.

We tried to get some order in our lives despite the war raging around us. We had oil heat in our tents but dared not open the damper at night because any light drew enemy fire. We had only a quart of water daily because the trip to the water point was hazardous. Showers were in an open tent for one hour each week. Most of us bathed in our helmet, when we dared take it off. We then washed our clothes in the same water. Most civilians had left the beachhead, and this forced us to do our own laundry. Wet laundry hung on the line across the tent daily. Those fortunate enough to find someone to do their laundry often had their clothes returned in shreds from bomb and shell fragments. Even laundry hung out to dry attracted enemy fire.

"I'm so glad it's cloudy today," I said to Mary one day in early March. "The clouds don't help my morale, but it'll stop Jerry from raiding today."

"They can still shell us, and that bothers me more," said Mary. "We have some warning with an air raid, but none with shelling." There were no attractive choices at Anzio.

Soon signs of spring came even at Anzio. Daylight hours lengthened and sea breezes carried tinges of warmth.

"I'm tired of wearing boots, wool pants, and shirt. I need a change." I pulled a pair of brown oxfords and a brown-and-white seersucker wrap-around dress from my barracks bag.

"Might as well wear our new clothes," said Mary. "Maybe we won't get another chance."

Mary's usual positive attitude had a trace of despair, and it bothered me. I realized for the first time that Mary was near exhaustion from the grueling duty in the operating room.

"It'll feel good to dress up," I said, trying to brighten the atmosphere. "I hope I won't freeze before I get off duty. The pants are a lot warmer."

Ambulance dug in for protection from bombs and shells

I dashed outside the tent. I had gone about a hundred feet when the frantic warning, "Incoming shell!" sounded over the public address system. I felt the percussion of shells falling in the hospital area. I fell to the ground and pressed my body into the damp sand and prayed I could get even lower. After a few seconds the explosions stopped. I ran a few steps and they started again. I had to hit the ground four times before I reached the ward, badly rumpled and covered with sand.

"You look so nice today," said the first soldier I met. "I like to see a woman in a dress." Many others expressed the same sentiment.

"It's a beautiful day. I didn't realize it would be chilly and damp out of the sunshine. I should've worn my new woolen sweater."

"Take my jacket," said an airman who had a traumatic amputation of the foot. He had suffered the wound during a raid to bomb Germany. His plane had been shot down over Brenner Pass in northern Italy.

"Oh, I can't," I protested. "You may need it."

"I won't need it for a while," he said. "If I ever get to fly again, the air force will give me another one." I cherished the brown leather jacket and wore it every time it rained.

The nurses were on the beachhead to care for the wounded. All the men, including the wounded, protected and cared for us in every possible way.

There were no further German offensives in March. Their attempts to push us from the beachhead failed. They concentrated on shelling and bombing instead because troops, ammunition, artillery, and supplies packed the area. They kept us under close observation and chose their targets well. Even mealtime was hazardous. Any concentration of people drew enemy fire. The shelling exhumed bodies in the cemetery and required the sad task of reburial.

The ditch beside the hospital took on the appearance of an underground city. Foxholes and bunkers honeycombed the bank. Many were elaborate, with tables and stools made from ration boxes. Others found furnishing in the surrounding homes. We could not take advantage of these shelters while on duty in the wards, but they did save the lives of those who used them.

A group of men used their ingenuity and fashioned a still from parts salvaged from wrecked equipment. Green wine, sold by a few remaining civilians on the beachhead, provided the basis for the concoction. The colorless liquid they produced was quite lethal, but many were willing to take their chances and drank it.

There was no letup in the number of patients admitted to the hospital. Adding to the wounded, many soldiers suffered exhaustion from the fierce fighting. We had two wards of thirty-six beds each filled with men who were emotionally unable to function. Some cried and others were silent. A few needed restraints for their transport to Naples for treatment. A condition called the "Anzio Shakes" claimed many victims. Those affected shook uncontrollably during an air raid or shelling. A few days rest, warm clothing, and food usually returned the patient to normal. I soon found out about this affliction firsthand.

The constant shelling and bombing caused some men to go off the deep end in other ways. I did a tour of duty in late March on a ward where fifteen men had self-inflicted wounds, mostly in the foot. The wounds were serious and recovery was slow, but most would not suffer permanent crippling. It was easy to understand the desperation that these men felt, even though the act was a war crime. They returned to the States for their long convalescence and their fighting days were over.

It was a rare treat for Mary and me to spend the evening together. On one such occasion, she said, "Major Larsen did a dramatic case today. He found a piece of shrapnel stuck in the aorta when he operated on a patient with an abdominal wound." The aorta is the largest vessel in the body and the shrapnel acted as a cork in a hole. Removal outside surgery would result in immediate death.

"It's a miracle he didn't bleed to death. Do you think he'll live?" I asked.

"He was doing okay when he left surgery," said Mary. "He's heavily sedated because they want to keep his blood pressure down."

"We'd better pray we don't have any air raids for a few days for his sake." Everyone in the hospital heard about the case and prayed for the soldier's recovery.

Casualties mounted among the hospital personnel. Nick, our first patient at Bizerte, was a victim of a bomb fragment to his lower abdomen. Like many wounds from metal fragments, a small puncture in the skin concealed extensive internal injuries. Nick's condition deteriorated rapidly and we soon knew he was infected with gas gangrene. Due to the location of the wound, little could be done to save his life. Men in receiving made a pine coffin for his burial. We gathered around the ambulance that bore his body while the bugler played "Taps." Once more, we said a sad good-bye to one of our own.

There was no rear area; the German guns reached every inch of the beachhead and harbor. Everyone was vulnerable to attack from the deadly shelling and bombing. Patients with minor wounds walked to the hospital. Others with serious wounds lived because the hospital was close to the front. I was less fearful for my life when I was on the wards surrounded by patients and fellow workers. I felt that the Germans directed every bomb and shell toward me when I was alone in my small wall tent.

Mail from home was the highlight of our days. I was grateful for my big family and they wrote faithfully. Letters from Mother especially warmed my heart, and I wished I could ease her worry about me.

When a package came in the middle of March along with the letters, I hurried to my tent and tore open the package. "Oh, look!" I said to Mary. "The olive-drab yarn I asked for nine months ago finally got here."

"What are you going to do with it?" asked Mary.

"I'm going to knit a sweater because I'm tired of freezing. Do you think the colonel will let me wear it?"

"It's the right color, so he shouldn't object," said Mary.

"Maybe I won't hear the shells if I'm counting stitches. I need something to calm my nerves."

I cast on the stitches and planned to start knitting when I went on night duty in a few days. Explosions and shells sounded closer and deadlier at night.

The shelling started at 0400 hours on March 22. Like clockwork, at two-second intervals, eighty-eight-millimeter shells "walked" toward us. I lay paralyzed with fright as the bursts passed overhead toward Anzio. About forty shells fell in the hospital area and the 15th Evac suffered the heaviest damage. One hospital ward received a direct hit that killed seven patients and wounded many others. Sandbags fortified some tents at the 15th, and this saved many lives. Steel fragments did not pass through the bags even when the shells landed close. Officials made plans to surround our hospital tents with sandbags. Finding sand was not a problem because we were on the beach. We abandoned any notion that the red crosses marking the hospital area offered a measure of protection.

The next few days included preparations for a visit from Gen. Mark Clark, commander of the Fifth Army, on March 29. (Jon said soldiers called him "Mark Time" Clark for failing to seize the opportunity to move off the beachhead during the invasion). We carefully lined cots, folded blankets, and picked up every scrap of paper on the ground in case the general visited our ward.

The general started his tour at 1530 hours and immediately the red alert sounded. He arrived without a helmet and someone in receiving rushed to get him one. Three Luftwaffe planes flew low and directly over the hospital as if putting on a special show for the general. It further confirmed our belief that nothing escaped German observation. Axis Sally gave a report of the day's activities and accurately named those involved. Would the Germans again try to push us into the sea?

The answer came just after dark when the dreaded red alert sounded. Planes swarmed overhead and dropped red, green, and white flares. This was the heaviest raid yet, and what did the colored flares mean? We speculated that it was to illuminate the hospital area. Our antiaircraft gunners hesitated to fire over the hospital for fear that falling flak would injure patients. One flare fell on the red cross in the center of the compound and lit the entire hospital area brighter than day. The sky burst with thunderous explosions from heavy antiaircraft guns with red tracer bullets. Searchlights added to the fireworks. I ran to the air-raid shelter and found it crowded with officers, nurses, and enlisted men. Once inside the shelter, I started shaking and couldn't stop. Bombs screeched earthward. I took a short, painful breath when I knew that they had not hit the shelter.

"Are you all right?" asked a soldier.

"I'm sc-scared," I replied, my voice shaking. "I c-can't stop shaking." I bit my lip and took a deep breath but I still shook. I now knew firsthand about Anzio Shakes.

The soldier put his arm around my shoulders and I was grateful for the added strength and comfort.

We emerged from the shelter an hour and a half later. Devastation was everywhere. The bombs had shredded canvas and scattered broken tent poles and personal belongings throughout the nurses' and officers' area. Bomb craters replaced tents. Incendiary bombs ignited fires, which the men quickly extinguished by scooping sand on them. Anxious voices filled the sudden quiet as we searched for friends. A bomb exploded just outside a ward tent killing four patients and wounding nineteen of the already wounded. Among the dead was the soldier operated on a few days earlier with shrapnel in his aorta. Twenty-one of our hospital personnel suffered wounds, among them two nurses. A big bomb crater shredded the huge red cross laid out in the center of the compound. Nerves, already raw, were stretched to the breaking point.

I went to bed fully clothed after the big raid and dozed while shells roared overhead all night. I took a deep breath after I realized they were landing beyond the hospital. There was no place to work in safety and it was especially hazardous for patients.

After General Clark's visit, officials decided to dig the hospital below ground to a depth of thirty-six inches. The 36th Engineers dug holes the size of each ward tent, berming the sand outside. They reinforced the walls of the excavations with chicken wire and a double row of sandbags. Sandbags divided each ward into three sections. This reduced the number of casualties in case a shell or bomb landed inside the tent. Timbers covered the operating room to offer some protection from falling flak. Double rows of sandbags and "flak shacks"—plywood canopies over each cot—protected nurses and officers. Most of the enlisted personnel dug their own foxholes, some quite elaborate. The engineers worked feverishly to complete the job before another devastating air raid. Since we were on the beach, there was plenty of sand, and they finished the project in a few days. We felt safer but continued to suffer casualties among our personnel.

The Anzio Express still roared overhead but we did have a much greater sense of security. Axis Sally taunted us daily with her broadcasts, referring to the beachhead as a large self-contained "Rest Camp."

Some of the men at the hospital gathered for a game of football on a balmy evening in late March. Almost immediately, the honey-toned voice of Axis Sally started her broadcast.

"Hi, fellas of the 56th Evac. I hope you're enjoying the ball game and your camp." It was chilling to know she was watching.

Almost immediately, shells began falling on the ball field. A shell hit the patient's mess and killed Private Early instantly while he worked there. Stoves, pots, and pans flew everywhere. Dirt from the explosion covered some of the ball players.

When would it end? There was no hope of reaching Rome, only twenty miles away, until troops from the southern front broke through the Gustav line and rescued us. Our spirits sagged with each tragedy in our ranks. Noisy nights made rest difficult, and it began to show in our sad, distraught faces. My trousers bagged and I realized how much weight I'd lost. Even my shoes were too big. I prayed to the Almighty for strength and protection.

It was time for another tour of night duty. I wanted to start the sweater during the long, early morning hours.

The patients were sleeping when the crash of an artillery shell shattered the uneasy quiet. A closer one was followed by yet another, even closer. I stood momentarily in the middle of the ward, afraid to move and afraid to stand still. The ward was full of men with plaster casts on their arms and legs. The most critically wounded patient lay on a hospital bed near the desk. His whole body, except his head and feet, was in a plaster cast. I wanted to cry for mercy.

"Please get under my bed!" said the soldier in the body cast.

"I can't do that. I'll be all right."

"You shouldn't take any chances. This plaster will protect me and we don't want you to get hurt."

Even though the soldier could not move, he wanted to protect me.

I took my knitting and sat on the ground with my back against the sand-bags. I knitted furiously until the shelling stopped.

I heard Jon come on the ward and ask the attendant, "Where is she?"

He pointed, and when Jon saw me, he slapped his forehead.

"I thought I'd seen everything," he said, " but never anything like this." Each of us found our own way to cope with the fiery cauldron around us. Many times, long after we'd left the beachhead, I heard Jon tell how I was knitting while the Germans shelled the hospital.

Ernie Pyle visited us often and his column appeared daily in the *Stars and Stripes* and newspapers at home. Other frequent visitors included Wick Fowler and Gens. Mark Clark, Lucien Truscott, and Whitey Lucas. Fifth Army Chief Nurse Lieutenant Colonel Wharton came to the hospital several times during our beachhead days to offer encouragement.

We developed a comradeship with our fellow workers, and at night the ties drew us even closer. I was walking to my tent following a night of duty in early April when I met Cpl. Pete Betley, a friend who worked in the laboratory. The Germans shelled installations around the hospital all night and our navy responded by sending shells over our heads toward the German lines. Meeting someone I knew well comforted me.

"Thank goodness, that night is over," I said. "It was one of the worst ones yet because there wasn't a quiet moment."

"None of the shells fell in the hospital area, although some were pretty close," said Pete.

"It looks like Jerry isn't going to give up before we're all killed or wounded." I could barely hide the despair that filled every fiber of my being.

"Just be sure to get into a foxhole when the shelling starts," said Pete.

"I feel a little safer since the engineers dug the hospital underground and sandbagged it."

"There's no doubt it helps," said Pete.

"Right now, I just want to sleep," I said as we parted. "I'll see you tonight."

I had been in my tent about twenty minutes when the frantic announcement, "Incoming shells!" blasted over the PA. I lay on the ground between the cots and prayed the sandbags around my tent would protect me.

During a pause in the shelling, I heard voices choked with emotion saying something about enlisted men. I knew a tragedy had happened. I ran to a group of soldiers just outside the nurses' area, "Was someone hurt?" I cried.

"Pete Betley," said one. "A shell landed in his foxhole and blew off both his legs at the hip."

"I talked to him just a few minutes ago," I said, choking back a sob. I grabbed the arm of a soldier to steady myself. Numbed with grief, I refused to believe what I heard.

"He was in his foxhole shining his shoes," said one of the soldiers.

We stood for a few moments, unable to find words that expressed our shock and grief. "That shell had his name on it," said one of the men finally.

I went to my tent, threw myself on the cot, and prayed through tears, "Dear God, don't let me be wounded like Pete. I'd rather be killed if a bomb or shell comes my way. Take care of Pete. Please God, protect us because I want to go home again." I fell asleep sobbing for mercy and did not awaken until suppertime.

The Germans shelled the hospital three times and bombed it once in the next three days. The stress showed on everyone. Weary eyes stared out of haggard faces. We could not conceal the strain. We looked old and felt tired. Those who once buoyed others with their cheery outlook no longer smiled.

Pete's condition improved and his heroic courage and fight for survival inspired all of us to carry on. We realized even more how closely we walked with danger and death. When would this terrifying episode end? Only twenty miles from Rome, but would we ever get there? Why did the Germans bomb and shell the hospital when they had a panoramic view of the beachhead from the hills? Troops and supplies packed every inch of the beachhead. Our rational thoughts told us it was impossible to miss the hospital when a shell missed its target.

Axis Sally started her program on April 6 by saying, "Happy days are here again for the 56th Evac. You'll soon be leaving the beachhead and I'm dedicating my program to you as a parting gift." What did she mean? How could she know this when we had heard nothing about it?

When I saw Jon, I asked, "What about this announcement Axis Sally made this morning?"

"Orders just came in for us to leave Sunday. We won't admit any patients after 1900 hour tonight."

Axis Sally had prophesied the truth and it stunned us. We had prayed continually for relief from the hazardous duty, but not by leaving the beachhead before we finished the job. No one wanted to be a quitter. We had lived like prairie dogs scurrying from one hole to another for so long it was difficult to imagine living in the sun. The prospect dazzled us momentarily. We had survived more than five hundred air raids along with shellings day and night for the past two months and a half. More importantly, we had cared for thousands of wounded and sick.

The 38th Evacuation Hospital, another 750-bed organization, would relieve us at 1000 hours on Easter Sunday. After an exchange of supplies and equipment, we would take over their facilities at Nocelleto near the Cassino front.

Easter Sunday, April 9, dawned dull and dreary. A soft rain fell. We packed a few personal items in our musette bags and sat on our bedrolls while we waited for the 38th. They arrived on time. I envied their high spirits and fresh look. The strain of the past two months and a half showed in our group. Clothes hung on many who had lost weight. We looked haggard and unkempt compared to the well-groomed and happy troops of the 38th.

I had lost twenty pounds at Anzio and was conscious of my baggy clothes when I talked to a trim nurse from the 38th.

"I hope you won't have shelling and bombing while you're here."

"We'll be fine," she said. "We're glad to be back in the thick of it again. It's been quiet on the Cassino front and we were too far back to receive casualties."

"The sandbags around the tents make everyone a little safer. Even so, always wear your helmet, because the shells come without warning."

"I will, and now I hope you folks can get some rest. We've been thinking about you and praying for you." Her kind words made me realize everything could be all right.

We climbed aboard the trucks for the ride down Purple Heart Alley to a ship waiting in the harbor to take us back to Naples. It was the first trip to the front gate of the hospital for most since we'd arrived in January. Only a few patients, among them Pete, were still in the hospital. We hated to leave them behind. Many familiar faces were missing. I was leaving some of my heart at Anzio. I turned my eyes toward the cemetery filled with marked graves. I said a prayerful farewell to Ellen, Gertrude, Rita, Nick, and thousands of others who had lost their lives on the beachhead.

The small towns of Anzio and Nettuno were now piles of rubble. The umbrella of silver barrage balloons over the harbor was thicker than before. Because the sea was too choppy for us to board the LST directly, we hurried aboard a waiting barge. It pulled away from the dock in record time as soon as the last man was on deck. The Germans lobbed a few shells in the water around us and sent tall sprays into the air. We were grateful for the protection of the navy destroyer that fired back. After trying several times to board the LST with a ramp, we once again climbed a Jacob's ladder to the waiting ship. The ship moved quickly out of range of the guns when everyone was aboard. Never had there been so many happy smiles of relief after being so close to death for the past few months. In spite of the rain, Providence smiled upon us. It was a glorious Easter Sunday for the 56th. The bare canvas bunks were luxurious and C rations had never tasted better. The gentle rolling of the ship and the swish of water against her sides lulled us into the most restful sleep we'd enjoyed in months.

We arrived in Pozzuoli the next morning. The sun shone, flowers bloomed, the grass was green—spring had arrived! We waited on the sea wall for trucks to take us to Nocelleto, where we took over the hospital the 38th had just left. I never ceased thanking God that I had survived Anzio.

Chapter XIII

Nocelleto

Our new camp was in a broad, green valley surrounded by steep mountains that glowed lavender when the sun sank behind them. The 38th laid gravel paths throughout the camp. Stone-bordered flower beds of geraniums, snapdragons, and daisies produced a riot of color at every intersection. The bedpan and urinal racks in front of each ward tent had a fresh coat of white paint. Flowering shrubs added more color to the glorious spring landscape. A forsythia bush was in full bloom outside the tent that Mary and I shared.

"This place is so beautiful. I don't want to move again until the war is over," I said to Mary. "What're you going to do tonight?"

"I think Dick will come over," said Mary. "We're getting married as soon as the war is over and we've a lot to talk about."

"I'm going to stay here and go to bed early," I said. "I want to enjoy a long night without red alerts or the Anzio Express."

171

The bugle call for dinner sounded over the PA. "We'd better go eat before the visitors arrive," said Mary. "I'm sure word got around fast that the 56th is back."

The mess hall was the usual long ward tent, but this one was luxurious, with wooden floors and potted plants. We heard the happy chatter and laughter before we reached the tent. Spirits were high and we reveled in being out of range of German artillery. The C rations had never tasted so good. An Italian civilian, Luigi, a man about thirty years old, waited on tables and bussed our dishes.

Mary and I were walking back to our tent when I heard over the PA: "Lieutenant Dagit, please come to headquarters."

Jack was waiting at headquarters. "It's great to see you," he said. "We watched and worried about you at Anzio. I found a little bar in a village near here. Let's go there and catch up on everything that happened for the past few months."

I hesitated, and then answered, "I suppose it's all right to leave camp for an hour or so."

"Of course, it is," said Jack. "What are you afraid of?"

"It's hard to get used to the freedom of moving around," I said. "We didn't go to the front gate the two and a half months at Anzio."

"There are no restrictions here, so let's go," replied Jack.

"I'd love to, but I do want to get home early and enjoy a long night's sleep."

While we drove through the countryside on the warm spring evening, I asked Jack, "What's happening here?"

"Everyone's getting ready for the big push on the Cassino Front," said Jack. "We'll hook up with Anzio forces. No one knows when it'll happen, but we're ready. We'll have enough troops and supplies to do the job this time. It'll be a short trip to Rome after the linkup."

I shuddered when I remembered how we thought it would be a short trip to Rome three months ago.

The bar was on a narrow street in a tiny village a few miles from camp. Army officers crowded the dark, noisy, smoke-filled room, making it hard to talk—but I enjoyed seeing Jack again.

It was dark when I returned to my tent. I rolled up the sides to let the spring breezes chase out the musty smell of the canvas. I carefully tucked the mosquito net under the edge of my sleeping bag to keep out the lizards. They were thick in the grass and I never got used to them crawling over everything.

We opened the hospital for patients on April 12, 1944. The front was quiet. Everyone waited for the big offensive to start. Most of our wounded were from artillery fire and patrols sent into enemy lines to scout their activity. Among the patients were soldiers from New Zealand, Canada, France, England, and the colorful Ghoums from French North Africa. Many of the patients on my ward suffered wounds to the extremities from small arms fire.

I was sitting at the desk filling out forms when I heard soldiers having a heated argument. When I walked toward them, one of the Americans said, "Watch what you're saying. Here comes the nurse." The argument escalated when the British soldier said that Americans were green and inexperienced. The British sprinkled their conversation with four-letter words that the soldiers did not want me to hear. We found our troops to be protective of us without fail.

Our first big event at Nocelleto was the celebration of our first anniversary overseas on April 24, 1944. Everyone was thankful to be alive and was in the mood for a party. The patient load was light, so everyone could attend the softball game between our nurses and the 95th Evac. Our team won easily. There was a baseball game later in the day between our hospital team and a neighboring ordnance unit. About a thousand friends and neighbors came to watch. Other activities included many impromptu acts on a small, outdoor wooden stage. Among the acts was a jitterbug exhibition by one of the enlisted men and a nurse.

We wore our new striped dresses and slacks, but some of us longed to dress in anything that was civilian. Colonel Blesse warned of a severe penalty if we were not always in uniform. I had a pair of brown pants I carried secretly in my barracks bag waiting for a chance to wear them. I said to Mary, "I'm going to wear my brown pants to the picnic tonight; are you?"

"No, mine don't fit too well," said Mary. "Aren't you afraid Colonel Blesse will see you?"

"I'll stay out of his way," I said. "Besides, he never notices me. His eyes are on some of the others."

We sat on the grass near the mess tent for the picnic. I was miserable trying to stay out of the colonel's sight. As soon as I had swallowed my last bite, I hurried to my tent and changed into brown-and-white regulation pants.

The celebration ended with a dance in the officers' mess. We decorated the hall for the gala party with with potted flowers and shrubs. The 175th Engineer band, friends from our early days in Tunisia, furnished the music. We shared drinks and toasted the memory of those missing since Anzio. Sam and I danced almost every dance until the party broke up in the wee hours of the morning.

The nurses started leaves at the Touristico Hotel in Naples a few days later. Mary and I, along with Lena and another nurse, Marge, were in the first group to make the trip.

"We'll have a chance to go to a real PX," I said to Mary while we packed for the trip. "Maybe we can find olive-drab dresses. I saw a nurse from another hospital wearing one at a party last week."

"I'd like to find a good tailor," said Mary. "I want him to make an Eisenhower jacket from one of my woolen ones."

"Colonel Blesse told Lena that the Eisenhower jacket is a regulation uniform," I said. "That would give us a little variety in our dress."

We arrived at the hotel just before dinnertime. After depositing our bags, we went to the beautiful dining room. We were welcomed by tables set with crystal glassware, fine china, and silver on white linen tablecloths. Strolling musicians went from table to table, stopping to play requests from the noisy diners. Our attentive waiter hovered over us, and the war was far away for the moment.

Lena stopped by while Mary was talking to friends at another table.

"What are you doing tonight, Avis?" she asked.

"Mary and I haven't decided yet."

"I thought maybe you'd go with Marge and me," said Lena. "We met some of the cast of *This Is the Army*. They found a little bar near the theater and want to take us there."

"I'd better stay with Mary tonight," I said. "Maybe tomorrow."

When we returned to our room, Mary began to repack her bag.

"Why are you packing?" I asked. "We just got here."

"I'm going to spend my leave with Dick at his apartment," said Mary. When she saw the look of dismay on my face, she added, "Don't worry. I'll be back in time to return to camp."

I sat on the edge of the bed after Mary left feeling sorry for myself. I felt that Mary had betrayed me by not telling me her plans. I had missed a good time because I had declined Lena's invitation. I was spending the first night of my leave in a hotel room alone.

The chugging sounds of German planes overhead jarred me to reality. Sirens wailed on all sides of the hotel. The lights went out, plunging my fourteenth-floor room into total darkness. My heart pounding, I raced into the hall. Bombs whistled earthward. I held my breath until I heard the thunderous crash nearby. The deafening blasts of the big navy guns joined the steady chatter of the ack-ack guns on shore. There wasn't a crack of light anywhere. I groped for the door that led to the stairs. I opened the door and tried to find the first step, afraid I would plunge down the stairs. I sat on the step and buried my head in my arms and cried. I was on the top floor. Who would find me if bombs landed on the hotel? The raid lasted an hour and a half. It one of the heaviest raids yet on the harbor, which was crowded with supplies for the push to Rome. When the lights came on, I found myself at the head of a steep flight of stairs. I returned to my room and slept on top of the covers, fully clothed, for the rest of the night.

I felt better when I awakened, but I was still annoyed at Mary and uncertain about how I would spend my leave.

When I reached the dining room, the first people I met were Lena and Marge.

"What'd you do last night?"asked Lena. Before I could answer, she went on, "You should've been with us. We had a wonderful time."

"I spent the evening alone, including the air raid," I said. "Mary is spending her time here with Dick at his apartment."

"You come with us," said Lena. "The fellows gave us tickets for *This Is the Army* this afternoon, and they want to take us out tonight."

"I'd love to join you, but won't three make a crowd?" I asked.

"Oh, no!" said Marge. "There are three of them and they're eager to get away from Irving Berlin for a while. They say he's so cross, and a relentless taskmaster."

We went to the show and loved it. It was fast-moving, humorous, and spoke a language we understood. We left the theater humming "This Is the Army, Mr. Jones."

Later in the evening, we found our way to a dimly lit bar in the basement of a bomb-wrecked building. Everyone crowded around a small table and the waiter brought a bottle of wine and six glasses.

"Could we please have another glass?" asked Lena soberly.

"We have six and that's one for each of us," said one of the men.

Lena turned the extra glass on its rim in the middle of the table and said, "This is in memory of Ellen."

We sat quietly for a few moments. I swallowed the lump in my throat and tears trickled down my cheeks.

We spent the next two days shopping all day and partying at night. I found an olive-drab rayon dress in the post exchange. A mirror hung in the makeshift dressing room, and I admired my reflection when I tried on the dress. I found a tailor on a narrow back street near the hotel and left my woolen jacket. With some gesturing and a few words of Italian, he understood that I wanted an Eisenhower jacket. The tailor cut off a regulation jacket at the waist and sewed a band at the waistline. These additions to my wardrobe gave my spirits a lift. I dreamed about buying colorful new clothes when the war ended. Civilian life was always near the surface in my thoughts.

We walked up and down every street near the hotel looking for something to buy. We found a few cameos of very poor quality, and paid an exorbitant price for them. Any piece of junk satisfied our longing to shop.

"Let's visit Pete tomorrow," I said to Lena and Marge. "He's in a station hospital here in Naples."

We set out for the hospital at 1000 hours the next morning. An old Italian woman in tattered black clothing was sitting on a corner near the hotel. She held a pail filled with bunches of daisies and snapdragons between her knees.

"*Quanta costa?*" I asked in my best Italian.

"One hundred lira," she replied.

"That dollar probably looks like a fortune to her," said Lena. "Poor woman, even when she has money, there's little to buy."

The station hospital was short distance beyond our hotel. When we approached the front door of a long brick building, Lena said, "This looks like a hospital in the States."

Inside, a corporal directed us to a twenty-four-bed ward where most of the patients were amputees. The sight of Pete, pale, with the covers lying flat on the bed below his hips, shocked me.

Lena, Marge, and I were tongue-tied for a few moments. I managed to say in a voice choked with emotion, "We brought you some flowers." I thrust the tiny bouquet toward him.

"I'm glad you came," said Pete weakly. "It gets a little lonely here."

"Are they taking good care of you?" asked Lena. "We'd give you extra special care if we worked here."

"Everyone has been wonderful, but I'll be glad when I get back to Minneapolis."

Conversation was difficult. I almost felt that I should apologize for my own wholeness of body.

"We'd better go," said Marge. "The cars are going to pick us up at one-thirty."

"We'll think about you when you're back in the States," said Lena. We walked back to the hotel, sobered by the sight of Pete and the enormous price he had paid.

Mary arrived at the hotel about twenty minutes before the cars came to take us back to camp. I was busy and I'd had a good time on leave, so I dismissed any thoughts of a confrontation with her.

We had few patients the next couple of weeks, and during this time Marlene Dietrich, Danny Thomas, and Irving Berlin each paid us a visit. We had movies almost nightly on a screen at the foot of a grassy knoll. Everyone attended, including the patients who were able. Those who needed help walking leaned on the strong arms of fellow soldiers. All the units around gave a party, and we had more invitations than we could accept. It was an uneasy calm because we knew the spring offensive would start at any time.

The evenings were long and warm in early May. I was on night duty and all the patients were at the movie. Capt. John Anderson, a family doctor in civilian life, came to the ward to visit. We talked about home and our lives before the army.

Eruption of Mt. Vesuvius in background

Jon came by each evening to bring the latest news. When he came in, Captain Anderson said, "I have to write letters tonight, so I'd better go."

"I know how that is. I always have letters to write," I said. "I'll see you tomorrow."

After Captain Anderson left, Jon said, "What was he doing here?"

He sounded jealous. I said, "He's lonely and just wanted to talk."

A few days later Jon said, "Captain Anderson is on his way home. He shipped out today."

The news stunned me. I asked, "What happened to him?"

"He lost his marbles," said Jon.

"What do you mean?" I asked. "He was fine a few days ago."

"He's depressed," said Jon. "He's been crying for two days and won't leave his cot. They're sending him back to the States."

Captain Anderson had seen the bodies of nurses killed at Anzio lying on litters and couldn't erase the picture from his mind. Anzio continued to claim its victims. Among them was Colonel Winans, our beloved chief of medicine, who had been one of the organizers of the 56th Evac. He returned to the States after developing coronary problems. Colonel Rippy, a kind and highly respected doctor, became chief. He proved to be a popular choice.

We wondered each day when the spring offensive would start.

Mary and I were getting ready for bed at 2300 hours on May 11 when we felt the ground tremble from thunderous blasts to the north. We ran outside and saw the horizon was ablaze with a red glow.

"It's started," said Mary, her voice choked with emotion. "The push has started."

I shuddered and said, "How can anyone survive that gunfire? I'm glad it isn't coming our way."

We stood speechless for ten minutes and watched. "Go get 'em, boys," said Mary. "We want to get this war over."

I thought about all the men I knew who were in the thick of the battle and it was hard to fall asleep. The roar of the guns gave me a chill even though we were several miles from the front.

The following Sunday was Mother's Day, May 14. I met Lena and Danny on our way to church services.

"Let's see if we can find a red flower," said Danny. "I always wear a red one because my mother is alive and well." We searched the flower beds and each found one.

We gathered at the chapel area where planks, supported on hollow tiles, served as pews. Major Willis was at the organ to lead us in song. As I sat in the warm spring sunshine, my mind drifted toward Mother and home.

Later the same day, the Germans raided the harbor at Naples. We felt safe from the daylight raid because we were more than twenty miles from the harbor. However, the all-too-familiar red alert and German planes overhead awakened us at 0300 hours. The sound of screaming bombs and explosions left no doubt that they were falling near the hospital. I rolled onto the ground and grabbed my helmet.

"Aren't they ever going to give up?" I said to Mary.

The plane made several passes over the area before the all clear sounded. We learned the next morning that the bombs had landed harmlessly on the baseball field.

Bombers filled the sky every day on their way north to bomb German installations in northern Italy and in Europe. Rail yards, oil fields, and ammunition dumps were their primary targets. The strength of the air force lifted our spirits.

We assembled near the flagpole in full uniform on May 15, 1944. Gen. Mark Clark came to award medals. He gave the hospital a Certificate of Commendation for our work at Anzio. He also awarded eighteen Bronze Stars for heroism and had a Purple Heart for Colonel Blesse. A muffled gasp went through the ranks when the colonel received his medal.

"When was he wounded?" I whispered to Danny.

"I heard he put in for wounds that he got at Bizerte."

"What kind of wounds? And where were they?"

"On his foot," said Danny.

"How did that happen?"

"He probably dropped a bottle of whiskey on it," answered Danny.

We regretted that some of the true heroes were not there to receive a medal.

The troops broke through the Gustav Line a week after the offensive started. They linked up with the troops from Anzio a few days later. We were far behind the lines and no longer received patients. We would soon leave the peaceful valley.

Chapter XIV

Fondi and Rome

We received orders on May 29 to move the hospital to Fondi, a small village thirty miles south of Rome. We were far behind the troops, who advanced rapidly each day.

"I'm glad we'll be closer to the front where we're needed," I said to Mary.

We helped each other roll our bedrolls packed with clothing. We gathered possessions after every move. Our barracks bags bulged with candles, shoes, knitting, old letters, and books. We hesitated to leave anything behind that might add to our comfort.

Maybe the war will be over in Italy when Rome falls, I thought. I tried to imagine the end of the war and thought dreamily of home.

"It shouldn't be long now before we're in Rome," I said to Mary.

Mary looked at her diamond engagement ring from Dick and I knew where her thoughts were at that moment.

It was several hours before the convoy of vehicles pulled into position for our trip north. Two soldiers helped us climb aboard the open trucks. It

Applying our makeup before boarding the trucks

was a warm spring day under a cloudless sky. We sang our usual songs, but
our enthusiasm for singing died after a few miles.

The convoy moved slowly along the ancient Appian Way. The highway,
begun in 312 B.C., extended from Brindisi on the Adriatic Sea to Rome. It
was now a thread of concrete in a man-made sea. The Germans had flooded
the Pontine Marshes to slow the advance of the Allied troops.

"Great job!" we shouted to a column of infantrymen marching south
along the road. "We're proud of you! Jerry is on the run now!"

The men were dirty and unshaven and their shoulders sagged under
the weight of their rifles. They looked like old men, but a closer look revealed
that they were very young. They waved and smiled when our truck passed.

We also met a column of German soldiers, guarded by Americans, going toward the rear.

"Those lucky guys will be going to the States," said someone. "That isn't fair."

We reached our hospital site in the early afternoon. Despite the fact that the hospital area was crowded between a dusty road and a grove of shell-shredded trees, no one complained. The front was moving rapidly north and that was more important. An advance detail of men set up showers in an open tent with a tarp stretched over the top. The nurses showered while the men set up our tents. Even though the water was cool, it was pure luxury to wash off the road dust.

Washing dishes—GI style

There wasn't a building in Fondi that had escaped the bombing and shelling. Former homes of the farmers in the area were now piles of rubble. The Italians retreated to the hills in droves to escape the *Tedeschi* (Germans) and were slowly starving. They had been living on boiled grasses for the past few months. A few were fortunate to have meat from a mule killed by a mine.

The kitchen was outdoors and we gathered with mess kits for the evening meal. We took our food and sat on the tarp spread out on the ground. Italian civilians of all ages packed the fence surrounding the mess area. They held pots, cans, and dishes toward us and begged for food.

"I can stand the older men watching me eat," said Mary, "but it really hurts to see the children."

"They're the ones who suffer most, and they didn't ask for any of this," I replied.

We scraped our mess kits before plunging them into the steaming barrels of soapy water and rinse. "I hate to throw this food away," I said to Mary, "but we might cause a riot if we give food to any of them."

I saw Jon later in the day. He said, "We had a pitiful case come to receiving this evening."

"Did one of the natives step on a mine?" I asked.

"An Italian woman came with a three-month-old baby," he said. "She's been nursing the child and her only food was boiled grass for many days."

"I wonder how they survived," I said. "Is the baby going to be all right?"

"He's severely dehydrated and malnourished," said Jon. "The poor baby looked like an old man with wrinkled skin. Major McCauley gave the mother some powdered milk and crackers."

Hospital officials made a plan to distribute leftovers when they realized how desperately the Italians needed food. Appetites diminished and everyone started asking for smaller servings.

We stayed close to camp for our own safety because the Germans had mined the area heavily. The Italians were not so fortunate and suffered many casualties from the mines. Most heartbreaking were the children. The wounds added to the stress of their malnourished bodies. Along with the human casualties was a heavy toll among the remaining livestock.

We had a small number of Allied wounded and injured from accidents the first three days the hospital was open. We were soon far behind the troops. We received orders to pack up and move again after seven days. The Allied troops entered the outskirts of Rome on June 4, 1944. Our next hospital site was in Rome.

We were up and packed several hours before the men loaded the trucks. The convoy was scheduled to leave at 1100 hours on June 6, 1944.

"I wonder what's holding things up?" said Lena. "I'm going to headquarters and find out when we're leaving."

"What's Lena so excited about?" said Mary. Lena was gone a few minutes before running back to where we waited.

"Great news!" said Lena. " The Allies invaded France this morning. General Eisenhower just made the announcement from his headquarters in England."

"The war should be over soon now," said someone.

"Maybe we won't have much to do in Rome. We'll have a chance to see some of the sights," said another.

"Did they say how the invasion was going?" I asked.

"No," said Lena. "It's a little too early to tell." I thought about the invasion at Anzio and said a silent prayer for the troops at Normandy.

Morale was high when the convoy left. We sang more lustily than on any trip yet.

"There should be good places to shop," I said to Lena. "I've had several requests for rosaries."

"I'd like to buy cameos for some of my friends in Kansas City," said Mary. "I'd rather see Saint Peter's Cathedral than shop, though."

Two dust-covered German bodies lay among the wrecked and burned vehicles that littered the roadside. I thought of the men's families in Germany. They also grieved for their fallen soldiers.

Bomb craters and a mass of twisted steel covered the rail yards on the outskirts of Rome. Well-fed and stylishly dressed Italians crowded the streets. Farther into the city, we saw little war damage. The crush of people around the trucks almost brought the convoy to a halt.

"The women don't pay much attention to us, do they?" said Danny. "They've got their eyes on the men."

"They've probably heard about American cigarettes and chocolate," I replied.

The convoy wound across the Tiber River, past the ancient Colosseum, Castel Sant' Angelo, the Roman Forum, and the Victor Emmanuel Monument. Saint Peter's Cathedral and the hills of Rome were lying on either side of the route. We were conquerors of the Eternal City riding triumphantly through the streets in the back of army trucks.

"Aren't we even going to stop here?" asked someone as we continued to move through the city.

"Maybe the troops are too far north already," said another.

"We can always come back here when the fighting is over," Mary said. "Let's just finish the war now while the Germans are on the run."

The convoy stopped on the western edge of Rome in front of Buon Pastore, a multiple-spired complex of buildings. The buildings were a former convent and had recently been used by the Germans as a hospital.

"We won't know how to act, living in buildings again after being in tents so long," I said to Mary. We climbed the stairs to our second-floor dormitory room where all the nurses shared quarters.

"It should be easier to set up the hospital, too," she replied.

We soon learned some of the drawbacks to buildings. The Germans had left quickly when the Allies closed in on them. We found half-eaten, freshly cooked hamburger patties and sauerkraut on plates at the table. The pot of beans on the stove was still warm. Instruments, syringes, and bandages that they'd left behind quickly disappeared for souvenirs. Two bodies were in the morgue. The buildings were filthy. We scrubbed and cleaned before opening the hospital for our first patients on June 8.

Litter bearers carried patients up steep, narrow stairs to the second floor. They carried them down again for evacuation to hospitals in the rear. We missed being at ground level where food, water, and supplies were a short distance away.

"It's easier to take care of patients in a tent," I said to Danny. "We could hang a bottle of plasma from the top of the tent and here I can't find an IV pole."

"Maybe we should be thankful the cots don't sink lower in the floor each day," she said. "That's about the only advantage I can think of."

We received hundreds of wounded the first week of operation. Many of the wounded were from the thousands of mines planted by the Germans. The cleverly concealed *Schuh* mines blew off the foot above the ankle when an unfortunate victim stepped on one of them. The "Bouncing Betty" was even more vicious; it wounded its victim in the buttocks and lower abdomen.

The number of wounded diminished rapidly after the first week and sightseeing was a high priority for everyone.

"The colonel is furnishing transportation for anyone who wants to go into the city today," said Mary. "We'd better go while we have a chance."

"I'm ready," I replied. "I'd like to get away from some of this bickering."

"What do you mean?"

"Betty accused Linda of bringing fleas to the dorm," I said. "I understand she took an Italian bus and the mohair seats were full of fleas."

"I'll be glad to get away for a while," said Mary. "There's a little too much togetherness when we're all in the same room."

Pope Pius XII scheduled an audience for the troops almost daily. The prospect of seeing the Pope thrilled me as much as it did Mary. I found a uniform without many wrinkles and buffed the dust from my shoes. Gathering all our rosaries and souvenir religious articles, we set out for the city. The doors to the Sistine Chapel were not open when we arrived and hundreds of soldiers pressed against the doors.

"There are two nurses here. Let them through," shouted someone. The crowd pushed us to the head of the line.

The doors opened and the crush of people continued to propel us forward. I found myself on the stage with Mary and five high-ranking officers.

Exploring Roman ruins

My heart raced, and I thought, *What am I doing here? I'm not Catholic. Will the Pope be able to tell?*

The door near the back of the chapel opened and the Pope appeared. Four Swiss Guards bore the Pope's white, canopy-covered carriage on their shoulders. He waved to the crowd as they proceeded down the aisle to the front of the chapel. He alighted and ascended the two steps to where Mary and I were standing. The Pope, dressed in a white robe and headpiece trimmed with gold braid, appeared frail.

He spoke in Italian, French, Arabic, and then in English: "Please raise your articles for blessing." He gave the blessing while everyone raised hands full of rosaries, medals, and crucifixes. Mary knelt and kissed his ring while I stood a few feet away. The guards lowered the carriage and the Pope seated himself. The guards carried him slowly down the aisle. He again waved to the crowd as he left the chapel. The audience lasted six or seven minutes. I felt equally blessed with everyone else present.

Our next stop was Saint Peter's Cathedral. I paused in the doorway and gazed at the enormous sanctuary filled with art treasures and statues.

"Where shall we start?" I asked Mary. "There's so much to see."

"Let's go clockwise from the main altar," she said. "We won't have time to see everything."

We studied the intricately carved marble statues of former popes. We brushed the toe of St. Peter with our lips. Thousands before us had followed the custom, and the toe on the dark statue was smooth and shiny.

Lt. Lena Grussing enjoying her new foot locker

After two hours in the cathedral, Mary said, "We still have time to go to the catacombs before our ride picks us up."

A little old Italian man met us in San Sebastian Church above the catacombs. We paid him ten lira, which equaled ten cents, and he led us to a small opening at the head of a steep stairs. We groped our way through the dark, damp, musty passages. Our guide, a pale monk in a brown robe, identified several small piles of bones excavated from the walls.

"I wonder if those bones really belonged to Whitey the Baptist," said Mary. We paused in front of a couple of long bones and fragments of smaller bones in one of the excavations.

"The early Christians sought protection from Mother Earth like we do now," I whispered to Mary.

We met our ride and went back to camp feeling that we had enjoyed an extraordinary day.

We returned to Rome at every chance because we knew our stay would be short. We liked to keep moving because each move meant we were closer to the end of the war. Days passed slowly, and we appreciated any break in the monotony.

A detail of men appeared at the door of our dormitory one afternoon. "We've got your footlockers," said one of them.

Our supply sergeant had found enough German lumber to make each officer and nurse a footlocker. The olive-drab boxes of rough lumber had our names, serial numbers, and shipping numbers stenciled on them. This surprise bit of luxury solved our furniture problem for the rest of the war.

After three weeks, orders came for us to move farther north. We made the move at night for the first time. Despite the hour, we started singing as soon as the trucks moved out in convoy.

Chapter XV

Piambino and Peciolli

We arrived at our new hospital site, a combination of wheat stubble and grape vines, at 0200 hours on August 5, 1944. An advance detail set up cots in pyramidal tents, eight nurses in each tent, for the rest of the night. No one wasted time getting to bed because we had to set up the hospital early the next morning.

The wounded swamped the hospital as soon it opened. Fighting for the port of Leghorn was some of the bloodiest of the Italian campaign. Soldiers suffered wounds as bad as we saw at Anzio, Avellino, and Dragoni. Supplies came through regularly, which made caring for casualties a little easier. Surgery operated around the clock.

Mary came to the tent in tears after a long, exhausting day in surgery. "Avis, some of the injuries were so bad, we could only clean their wounds," she said. "Three had their buttocks blown away by machine gun fire. The Germans spotted them when they crawled across an open field."

I sat quietly, unable to find words to express my anguish. I finally said, "I couldn't work in surgery. The patients on my ward have their wounds covered with plaster."

"Mac invited me to have a drink with him," said Mary. She got up and brushed away the tears. "I'll see you later."

Mary's drinking troubled me because that is where she often sought comfort. I hoped Dick would come before Mary had too many drinks. He came often because his outfit was only a few miles away.

The evenings were long and we went to the beach to watch the moon rise at every opportunity. The days were hot and the cool sea breeze refreshed us. Jack came by and we went to the nearby beach and for a ride through the countryside. Mary was in bed asleep when I returned to the tent.

The front moved forward, after two weeks of bitter fighting, and the flow of patients slowed dramatically. Everyone had days off and we took advantage of the luxury of being near broad, sandy beaches. Some had swimsuits from home and others wore anything they could find.

I was sitting on my cot, reading letters from home, when Mary came to the tent. She carried two white bath towels and a sewing machine from surgery.

"Nick wants to go swimming," she said, "and he doesn't have a swimsuit."

"Are you going to make him one?"

"I'm not," she replied. "I told him you could sew and would make it for him."

"I don't have a pattern," I protested.

"You don't need a pattern. I know you can do it."

I saw Nick a few days later, and he said, "The suit you made fits. Thank you so much. I've spent many hours at the beach in it."

I went to the beach many times but was cautious about exposure to the sun after my experience with sunburn in Casablanca. The endless ink-blue waters of the Tyrrhenian Sea cradled a deep, sandy beach.

I sat on the warm sand, covered with a towel, while others swam. Children romped, threw sand, giggled, and waded in the surf. I watched Italian women wriggle out of their swimsuits into street dress without exposing themselves. I thought dreamily of home and imagined women and children there on a warm summer day.

Army units returning from the front gave parties and invited the nurses. Several of us went to a party given by a 34th Infantry Battalion at a seaside villa. We spent the afternoon sailing, a new experience for me. It was windy and I didn't wear a life jacket and couldn't swim.

"If we capsize, just hang on to the boat," shouted someone above the noise of flapping sails.

I loved sailing and thought about the dangers only when we were safely back on shore.

We prepared to move because, after four weeks, we were far behind the front. We feared that we would be in the invasion of southern France because of our experience at Anzio. Instead, orders came to move the hospital north and inland, near the village of Peciolli, on August 30, 1944.

We expected this to be just another move in the back of a two-and-a-half ton truck. Instead it turned into a hair-raising experience. Our convoy had inexperienced drivers for a route through the most wildly rugged and scenic mountains in Italy. We climbed higher and higher over hairpin curves so sharp the trucks couldn't negotiate them in one turn. The driver turned, backed up, and proceeded with a jerk. We huddled together in the middle of the truck bed, afraid to look down at the steep, bottomless canyon a few feet away.

A small village hugged the summit of every mountain. Faded yellow stone buildings crowded both sides of the road. Italian women, men, and children stood in every doorway and watched us pass. Chickens and dogs fled for their lives. The truck came close to scraping the buildings on each side of the narrow road.

We pounded on the cab and shouted, "Slow down!" when the driver tried to make up lost time on the mountain curves.

It was an unpaved route and a choking cloud of dust enveloped us, obscuring the following truck. Away from the villages, the scenery was breathtaking, with rugged peaks and mountain streams. On every bank, Italian women scrubbed laundry on the rocks. Children skipped from boulder to boulder and paused to watch the convoy pass.

Our new camp was in a remote valley near Sienna and many other hilltop villages of ancient times. The hospital site was in an alfalfa field surrounded by vineyards and cypress trees.

We were covered with dust, and my auburn, curly hair hung stiff and straight. Some wore surgical masks or glasses for protection, and the outlines gave them an eerie appearance. We headed for the showers as soon as the trucks stopped. The warm water formed rivulets of mud on our bodies. It had never felt so good to arrive at our destination safely and to be clean.

We saw piles of German box mines along the road and soon learned their toll on both soldiers and civilians. We had barely reached camp when there was a thunderous explosion. An Italian farmer was working a nearby field with a team of oxen when one stepped on a mine and killed both oxen. The farmer suffered wounds, and our hospital took care of him. A few days later, a group of children were playing with a rifle grenade when it exploded. It blew off the hand of one little boy and seriously wounded six other children. The Germans used their imagination in sowing the mines. They often attached these wicked devices to an innocent-looking twig, producing disastrous results.

The wounded came to the hospital in overwhelming numbers. Among the wounded were Nisei (Japanese American) men of the 442nd Infantry Division. Despite their wounds, these men did not ask for sedation to ease

Typical medical ward scene

their pain. A soldier with both arms and one leg encased in plaster shifted restlessly on his cot.

"May I give you something for pain?" I asked.

He smiled weakly and said, "I'll be okay."

"I know you will," I said, "but a shot will make you feel better." He took the shot and soon fell sound asleep. Like the soldiers in the field, we admired these brave men.

The most common wound on my ward was traumatic amputation of the foot. The injury occurred when a soldier stepped on a *Schuh* mine. There were fifteen with this type of wound on the ward in one twenty-four-hour period. As bad as these wounds were, the soldiers felt fortunate to be alive and knew that their fighting days were over.

The troops moved slowly north and the Allies invaded southern France. General Eisenhower again predicted, optimistically, that the war would end in 1944. Our hospital admitted its fifty-thousandth patient. The end of the war couldn't come too soon. We waited eagerly for news of the troops crossing the Arno River and taking Florence.

Our patient load was light after a few weeks and we were anxious to explore the countryside.

"How would you like to go to Pisa with Dick and me today?" asked Mary.

"I'd love to," I said. "I was hoping to see the Leaning Tower before I left Italy."

We drove west, the mountains fading behind us as we approached the lowlands near the sea. We saw a few army vehicles on the narrow road that followed the coastline to Pisa. We were in an open Jeep and ocean breezes blew in my face on the warm, sunny fall day. Mary and Dick laughed and talked and I was alone with my thoughts. I thought about the approaching holidays and wondered how many more there would be before the war ended. I longed for an end to the suffering, seeing poor, begging Italians as well as ancient sites.

"We're here," called Mary.

I quickly turned my attention to reality. I hoped Mary and Dick could not read the thoughts that raced through my mind on the trip. Was I selfish? Perhaps not. Everyone dreamed of the day the war would end and we could go home again.

We got out of the Jeep and walked closer to the tower and baptistry.

It was a shock to see how far the tower leaned.

"It's a miracle all the bombing and gunfire didn't knock it down," said Dick. The Italians had removed all artifacts from the baptistry and tower for safekeeping. We did not see any civilians around and we were alone viewing this amazing structure. The tower had survived other wars and it appeared to have survived this war, too.

We took advantage of the lull in work and caught up with laundry and much needed sleep, our number-one pastime. We searched for creative ways to fill our days.

Danny came to me and said, "Let's go to Rome tomorrow."

"How can we do that?" I asked. "We'd have to get a leave to go that far."

"Betty and Ruth hitched a ride on a plane and went yesterday," said Danny.

"I'm willing to try it," I said. "We can get up early so we'll get a good start."

Danny and I went to the motor pool at 0700 hours the next morning.

A sergeant and corporal were getting into a Jeep. I ran toward them and called, "How about a ride to the airfield near here?"

"Sure," said the sergeant. "Hop in. We're headed that way."

When we arrived at the airfield, a C-47 on the runway was preparing to take off. Danny and I ran toward the plane shouting, "Wait for us!"

A soldier was ready to close the door when I asked breathlessly, "Are you going to Rome?"

"Yup, do you want a ride?"

We climbed aboard and seated ourselves on the steel benches that ran along each side of the cabin. The plane taxied down the runway and slowly left the ground.

The tree-covered mountains, laced with streams and ravines, almost touched the underbelly of the plane.

"This sure beats riding over the mountains in a truck," I said to Danny.

"I can't believe our luck," said Danny. "I hope we find a way back as easily."

"I'll ask the pilot when they're going back," I said. I went to the front of the cabin and asked, "Could we get a ride back later today?"

"Sure," replied the pilot. "We're picking up airplane parts, so come back in time for us to leave at 1630 hours."

"We'll be here," said Danny, and we ran to a Jeep leaving for the city.

It was 1200 hours when we reached the Piazza del Popolo and Via Veneto in downtown Rome. We searched several small side streets before we found the photographer where Betty and Ruth had had their picture taken.

"I wish I hadn't promised to pick up those pictures," said Danny. "It doesn't leave us much time to do anything else."

"Let's go to the PX," I said. "It's not far from here and we can get something to eat. I'm starved."

We had a hot dog on a dry bun and coffee before looking for something to buy. Danny and I each bought "army pink" wool skirts to go with our Eisenhower jackets, the chic uniform of the day. Our shopping was done and it was time to start looking for a ride back to the airfield.

A corporal and a captain were sitting in the first Jeep we saw when we stepped outside the PX. The captain got out of the Jeep and came over when he saw Danny and me deciding what to do next.

"Do you need a ride somewhere?" he asked.

"We have to be back at the hospital about thirty miles south of Florence today. Are you going near the airfield?"

"We'll take you there. Our headquarters are near the field."

"We really appreciate this ride," I said. "We've been lucky on this trip."

"Glad to give you a lift," said the captain. "Hope you make it back okay."

The return trip went as smoothly as it had in the morning.

A few days later Mary and another nurse went to Rome. Mary was quite drunk and without her shoes when she returned to our tent. Before I asked, she said, "My corns hurt so, I took off my shoes and I can't find them." She continued, "We had a great time and the pilot even let me fly the plane." When I heard this, I wondered if hitchhiking by plane was a good idea.

We integrated more refinements into our daily lives with each move. The public address system was put into operation first. Bugle calls, telephone messages, and visitor announcements blared throughout the camp.

Everyone knew when you had plans for the evening. The army issued two cartons of cigarettes to everyone each week. One carton was your choice of Camels, Chesterfields, or Lucky Strikes. The other carton was a little-known brand. We did not smoke the unpopular brands, but they were a treat for the Italians. We used them to barter for laundry service, shoe repair, tailoring, and wine. Mail came regularly and was the most popular of all bugle calls. Everyone received one bottle of Coca-Cola and spent considerable time contemplating how to make the most of the treat. Shortly after the Coke came a beer ration, which was a big hit with many. I gave mine to Mary. She often joked she was going to have a Budweiser pool when she got home and would swim in it every day. We danced on the wooden floor in the mess hall and a record player provided the music. We called the mess hall "The Tight Shoe Tavern" during these events.

We were in a blackout area and had an occasional red alert. It was usually one German plane that caused little excitement.

The long days created a problem for showing movies. Trees camouflaged the screen in a hollow at the foot of a knoll. We sat on the hillside hissing and booing when the projectionist changed reels. Despite technical problems, everyone loved American movies and home felt a little closer.

Jack, Bob, Ray, and other men I met in the service came by when they heard the 56th was in the area.

"What are you going to do if all these fellows show up the same evening?" asked Mary.

"I'll worry about that when it happens," I said. "They're all good friends and I'm not madly in love with any one of them."

"What about your boyfriend from home?"

"I'm not in love with him, either. I still write, and he's in Scotland now," I said. "We may see each other differently when the war is over."

"I'm dreaming of the day when the war is over. Dick and I can get married," Mary said serenely.

Many of the nurses had serious relationships with the men they met. I thought about the nurses who grieved when their man was transferred, killed, or wounded. Some gave their hearts to married men. I believed the war would end and I didn't want to go home with a broken heart.

We always looked for something to buy. This part of Italy was famous for its alabaster, a soft, white, semi-transparent stone. The Italians carved the stone into ashtrays, bookends, boxes, and animal figures.

When I saw Danny, she said, "Come to my tent and see what I bought." She showed me an elephant about the size of a football. "I'm going to send it to Mom and I know she'll love it."

"How are you going to wrap it?" I asked. "Aren't you afraid it'll get broken?"

"Ernie said he'd put a plaster cast around it for me," said Danny. "It'll be heavy but should get to South Dakota okay."

Danny heard from her mother a few weeks later. She had received the package, but both elephant and plaster cast were damaged beyond repair. This cooled our enthusiasm for mailing anything breakable home.

Locally grown vegetables, especially tomatoes, added some variety to our diet. Word spread quickly one day in early September that we would have fresh eggs for breakfast the next morning. We were up early, waiting in line, for two eggs prepared our favorite way. Bill, Paul, and Carl beamed when they served them and heard few complaints about lumpy oatmeal or cold coffee.

The troops met fierce fighting when they tried to cross the Arno River and enter Florence. The Arno line broke and fighting moved north of the city on September 15, 1944.

Chapter XVI

Scarperia

We received orders to move the hospital north of Florence on September 23, 1944. Each move north meant the end of the war in Italy was a little closer. The convoy wound slowly across endless mountains and streams on a bright fall day. The Germans blew every bridge when they retreated. Engineers built Bailey bridges, constructed of prefabricated steel parts bolted together like Erector sets. These bridges made it possible for the convoy to pass. The peaks became less rugged and we saw the outline of Florence in the distance.

As we came closer, we saw the Duomo looming above the red-tile roofs in Florence. The broad Arno River, the recent site of heavy fighting and a Hitler stronghold, ran through the center of town.

"I hope we stop here," I said to Danny. "This city doesn't look badly bombed except in the outskirts."

"I wonder what they have to sell?" she said. "I'd love to go shopping."

We skirted the city and proceeded twenty miles north. The convoy stopped near the small village of Scarperia in the foothills of the Apennines. The trucks left the highway and pulled into an open field. It was a potato patch and was the site of our next hospital area. The mountains appeared close enough to reach out and touch them.

We jumped from the trucks as soon as they stopped. The sun was sinking behind the mountains and the air was damp and chilly. Everyone was hungry and stiff from the four-hour trip from Peciolli. An advance detail of men had our tents ready.

I said to Mary while we walked to our tent, "I'm going to make up my cot before it gets dark. We should get electricity tomorrow."

"I'm not going to unpack much," said Mary. "We might not be here long."

"Let's go eat," I said. "Maybe someone has an idea how long it'll be before we move again."

Everyone soon forgot their disappointment about not stopping in Florence because the fighting was going well. We believed our troops would soon be in the Po Valley and Bologna was the last stronghold in Italy.

Speculation was rampant about our length of stay in the area. Morale was high because the cooks dug potatoes. We had real potatoes the first time in many months. They also made ice cream, and that added to the festive meal.

Heavy artillery surrounded the hospital area and the percussion from the firing almost blew out our candles. There was a feeling of security knowing the guns protected us, but they moved out after a few days. We admitted a steady stream of wounded as soon as the hospital opened. The Germans were on the higher elevations and made a desperate stand to protect the rich and fertile Po Valley.

Each day brought changes in the weather. We had many days of pouring rain and low clouds. The clouds prevented our air force from making

Hospital setup; mountains always loomed in the background

strikes on enemy troops and cities on the European continent. On an occasional clear day, our planes flew by the hundreds on bombing missions over
German cities.

We saw little of the German Luftwaffe for a few weeks and believed it
was no longer a serious threat. The drone of German planes overhead on
a moonlight night in October shocked our sense of complacency. The red
alert sounded over the PA at 2300 hours. Planes swooped and flew at tree-
top level over the hospital with their guns blazing. We prayed they could
see the hospital area in the moonlight. They raided all night along the road
past the hospital firing on ammunition dumps, supplies, and convoys. A
shell exploded in the enlisted men's area of the hospital near the road at
0430. The shell killed one of our men. The death of this popular soldier
saddened everyone. The men moved away from the highway the next day.
The Germans reminded us that the war was not over.

Our troops engaged in fierce fighting in the Apennines. They tried desperately to get into the Po Valley before winter. Many casualties were from hand-to-hand fighting. Others suffered multiple wounds from the thousands of mines sown by the Germans.

The days marched into fall and we saw the snow line moving farther down the mountainsides. Once again the Germans had denied us an end to the war in Italy. It became clear that the front had stalemated for several months to come.

The number of casualties slowed by late October, and we made our first trip to Florence. Danny and I walked around the Piazza della Signoria looking for an open shop. There was little to see because boards covered all the shop windows.

"Let's go down by the river and see if there's anything there," I said to Danny.

We picked our way through the rubble and came upon an old man in tattered black clothing. His shoulders stooped and tears streamed down his withered face. He searched among the huge cement boulders and twisted steel.

"What's he looking for?" I asked Danny.

"He won't find much here," she replied. "The Germans made sure of that."

He saw us and gestured by thrusting his arms above his head. *"Tedeschi! Tedeschi!"* he cried. He pointed to the blown bridges and his shoulders sank even lower. He repeated the word *casa* several times as he tried desperately to tell what happened. He wanted us to understand his pain. Even though we could not speak Italian, the man's grief touched us deeply. The Ponte Vecchio was the only ancient bridge standing across the Arno.

"I've seen enough of Florence today," said Danny. "I'm glad it's time to go back to camp."

Our patient census hovered around four hundred after the fighting stalemated. We admitted patients with wounds from small-arms fire suffered while on patrol duty. Others had colds, fever, or trench foot from sitting in foxholes half filled with water for days at a time. We now had penicillin. All wounded, in addition to those with colds, sore throats, or infections, received the drug. We gave it by intramuscular injection every four hours. The soldiers hated this treatment. Many patients said they preferred their chances at the front compared to a shot every four hours. The patient who complained the loudest had a sprained ankle!

Many patients complained of a severe cough, although I did not hear much coughing. I became suspicious when I realized we were using large amounts of elixir of terpin hydrate with codeine.

"Could you give me a glass of cough medicine and leave it by my cot?" said a young soldier. "If I cough during the night, I won't need to call you."

"I don't mind if you call me," I said. "I'm here to get what you need."

"We sure use a lot of cough medicine," I said to Major Nelson, the ward officer. "The patient in bed twenty-two wants a whole glass full."

"You know why, don't you?" he replied. "That medicine is almost pure alcohol and it's like a shot of whiskey."

We had a few severely wounded men and we hovered over them. We watched for signs of sensation in the fingers of a soldier with a shattered shoulder and severed nerves to his arm. An eighteen-year-old suffered an abdominal wound his first day on the battle lines. He had a colostomy and developed pneumonia. We encouraged him to cough and held his hand when he cried with pain. All the critically wounded needed encouragement, and we listened when they wanted to talk to someone who understood. They were sorry to leave our hospital because they knew they would not get so much special attention again.

When we realized we would not be moving for several months, we tried to make our tents as homelike as possible. We had electricity and a bare bulb hanging in the center of the tent. An oil-burning potbelly stove kept the tent cozy and warm. Wooden floors, four-foot-high sides, and a door gave each tent unusual comfort. A friend gave Mary unbleached muslin and we lined the tent roof to reflect light. We cut a green satin spread from home in two pieces for cot-sized spreads. Ration boxes furnished us with table-top space. In spite of these luxuries, we examined our possessions and often found them covered with green mildew. When Mary took her brown leather purse from the barracks bag one evening, it was a light pea green.

"Well, that takes care of this purse," she said angrily. She opened the door and tossed it outside.

"We can remove the mildew with warm water and soap," I said.

"No, we can't," she snapped. "I'll never use it again."

While Mary was at the latrine later in the evening, I retrieved the purse and put it under my cot. I cleaned it and gave it to her later when she was in a good mood. She used it until the end of the war.

One of our most prized possessions was a gallon can from the mess. We heated water for baths and washing our hose. Jon found us a good laundry woman to wash the heavy shirts and underwear. Our shower facilities were in a tent and the only heat came from the water. Clouds of steam billowed around us when we showered. We often found a bath in a helmet full of warm water refreshing. We used the water later to remove mud from our boots.

The longer we were overseas, the greater our hair problems became. I watched to see who was handiest with a pair of bandage scissors. I discovered Marge gave a fairly good haircut, and we used the outdoors for a beauty salon. Some who'd had permanents before they left the States now had a three-inch fringe of curls on shoulder-length hair after two years overseas. A turban fash-ioned from an olive-drab handkerchief covered many hair problems.

We longed for something civilian to wear. The colonel warned we should not not even think of wearing anything but regulation uniforms. Despite the warnings, I wrote home to Leona and asked her to buy brown pumps for Mary and me. We tucked a bag, with the pumps, discreetly under our arm every time we left camp. When we were safely out of sight, we changed from our plain brown regulation army oxfords. The idea of getting by with something meant even more than the change of shoes.

We took advantage of the quiet time and broadened our social activities. There were many parties, both at the hospital and with army units returning from the front. Jack and Bob came by when they were in the area and shared candy, nuts, and cookies from home. An evening in the tent alone was almost a treat.

Mary and I continued to knit olive-drab sweaters. She knitted for Dick and I knitted for myself because I went out with many different men. We took turns reading aloud from works by Robert Penn Warren, H. Allen Smith, and James Thurber while the other knitted.

Like all army units, we had many talented and educated people among our personnel. One of enlisted men started a library. He gathered paperback books and comic books ("Major Mighty" was the soldiers' favorite). Any reading material he found, along with newspapers from home, filled the shelves. Books, especially comics, fell apart quickly. Pages critical to the story were often missing, but we still read them.

The Fifth Army provided a rest hotel for nurses near the center of Florence. We went in groups of six and everyone had a leave there in November. The hotel was a well-preserved European-style hotel, one of many in Florence, and most served as rest hotels for military personnel. We arrived at the hotel just before dark. Army officers waiting for friends, or to check on the new arrivals, lounged in the small lobby on first floor. A large dining room off the lobby, set with white tablecloths and silver, promised the usual mealtime treat.

Gwen Allen from Fort Worth, Texas, and I shared a third-floor room. We unpacked our bags, mostly underwear, and enjoyed the luxury of a dresser. It took only a few moments to adjust to our comfortable accommodations.

"What are your plans for tonight?" I asked Gwen.

"I have a date with Gordon Hall. He's with an antiaircraft outfit and is coming down with a friend."

"My friend from the antiaircraft is coming, too. I wonder if they know each other."

We discovered that Gordon and Dan Connors, my date, were good friends. Their outfit, stationed at the foot of the Apennines, was about thirty miles north of Florence.

We soaked in the tub before dressing for dinner. The highlights of any trip to a rest hotel were a bathroom and real beds with mattresses.

Attentive Italian waiters met us at the door of the dining room. Musicians with violin, accordion, and clarinet strolled among the tables. They serenaded us with "That's Amore," "Funiculi, Fenicula," "O Sole Mio," and other familiar tunes while we ate. We kept our waiter busy bringing baskets of hard rolls. They tasted like dessert after heavy army bread.

Dan and Gordon came the first evening to take us dancing at their officers' club. A spacious brick villa owned by an aristocratic Italian family served as an officers' club for antiaircraft personnel. A high stone wall surrounded the villa and grounds on the outskirts of Florence.

The sentry, a soldier, stood guard at the gate. It was dark and we groped single file through garden paths to the door of the mansion. We heard band music before we reached the door. A twenty-piece band filled a stage at one end of the former spacious dining room. Officers crowded around a bar at the other end of the room. The air was blue with smoke. A noisy crowd of officers and their dates did not detract from the music of popular tunes from home. Many of the musicians had been with big-name bands before the war. I forgot for a moment where I was when they played "Stardust," "Sunrise Serenade," and "I'll Be Around." We danced until the band played

*Lts. Duffy DuPont, Frances Raymond, Gwen
Alsup, and Avis Dagit on leave in Florence*

"Good night, Sweetheart" at 0130 hours. Gwen and I attended many Saturday night dances with Dan and Gordon the next few months.

While we were at Peciolli, a rumor circulated that there would be a ration of American liquor for the officers. American troops always looked for liquor and some made mental plans for their ration. None of the nurses got any liquor and the rumor quickly died. It mattered little to me.

A group of nurses gathered in the mess hall for supper a few weeks later. "Did you know the liquor ration came?" said a nurse who dated one of the doctors.

"Where's ours?" asked someone.

"The captain in supply decided it should be for the male officers," was the reply.

"Are they trying to get by with something?" said another.

"We're officers, too, and I want mine," chimed in another. "I'll decide for myself what to do with it."

Each nurse received a ration of American liquor a few days later. We did not share it with the male officers because they had kept the first ration for themselves.

Everyone had a chance to vote in the presidential election in November. President Roosevelt was the only president I had ever voted for, so I did not have a problem deciding how to vote. We were barely aware of his opponent and felt it was a poor time to change leadership.

Jon and I saw each other almost daily. Others came and went, but I depended on his being there day after day. When he said, "Avis, you mean more to me than anyone in the world," I was a little frightened and confused. I did not want my heart to rule my head. I knew Jon was married.

"Please don't say that," I said. "Maybe we shouldn't see each other so much."

"I wanted you to know how I feel," he said.

I sat quietly for a few moments before I said, "You're important to me, too, but I just want to be friends."

A few days later Jon came to my tent with a pair of German binoculars and a German Luger he had taken from a prisoner in receiving. "Would you keep these for me?" he asked. "I received orders for a three-month furlough in the States."

"That's wonderful," I exclaimed. "I'm sure you're anxious to see your new son."

"I'm not excited about a trip home," he said. "If I don't come back, the binoculars and gun are yours."

"Maybe the war will be over and you won't have to come back."

There was a little ache in my heart when I buried the souvenirs deep inside my barracks bag. I missed Jon and his help in solving day-to-day problems. He found a laundry woman, made sure I had my favorite brand of cigarettes, and brought the latest news. I wasn't lonely, however, because there were many parties and I looked forward to a date with Dan each Saturday night.

Gwen and I were ready when Dan and Gordon came from their posts farther north in the foothills in early December. We felt safe when Corporal Drew drove because of his experience in blackout driving. We piled into the Jeep for the twenty-mile drive down the winding road to the club. It was a moonless night and the road was soft from recent rains. We had gone about ten miles when we felt the Jeep pull slowly to the side. Before anyone could say anything, the vehicle tipped. We leaped clear while the Jeep came to a stop on its side in the shallow ditch.

"Are you okay?" asked Dan anxiously.

"Is anyone hurt?" said Gordon.

No one had injuries. One of the men said, "Let's put this Jeep back on the road."

The three men lifted the vehicle and turned it on its wheels. We seated ourselves again and went to Florence for an evening of dancing.

Our second holiday season overseas approached and everyone made plans for the celebration. Spirits were high despite the news from Europe where our troops were fighting the Battle of the Bulge in Belgium. We would not allow ourselves to wallow in self-pity like we did the year before at Dragoni. We had a bountiful feast at Thanksgiving with turkey and all the trimmings. Following that holiday, our thoughts turned to Christmas.

We stretched our creative talents to the maximum with our Christmas decorations. We stole ideas from others and tried to outdo those in neighboring tents. We pruned evergreen and holly boughs from trees in nearby farms and brought them to the hospital by Jeep loads. Doctors, nurses, ward attendants, and patients spent many hours making garlands and wreaths. We stripped leafless tress of their mistletoe and it, too, appeared in our decorations.

Colonel Blesse granted the nurses permission to give a Christmas party for the enlisted men of our hospital. Each nurse took five names and we shopped for gifts on one of our trips to Florence. There was little choice in merchandise, so most men received an Italian billfold. We made trays of candy, nuts, and cookies pooled from boxes we had received from home. Everyone drank punch made with our liquor ration and grapefruit juice. We danced a few steps with each man on a twelve-by-twelve-foot wooden floor in the noisy, smoke-filled tent. We had a party for the officers a few nights later, but we enjoyed the enlisted men's party more.

I went to Catholic mass with Mary on Christmas Eve and the Protestant services at 1000 hours the next morning. The tent was full of worshippers. We offered our thanks to God for protecting us thus far and prayed the war would end soon. Good-natured snowball fights broke out and tents sagged with the heavy snow that fell during the night. Spirits were high because we felt this would be our last Christmas overseas.

On New Year's Day, the Fifth Army and the air force played a football game in Florence. One of the Mussolini stadiums we called the Spaghetti Bowl was the site of the event. Gwen and I planned for many days to attend with Dan and Gordon.

While we waited for the men to arrive, I asked, "How are we going to keep warm?"

"I have some cognac we can mix with juice in our canteens," she said. "The fellows will have something too."

"I've got extra blankets we can take," I said.

New Year's Day was gray and chilly when Dan and Gordon arrived. We huddled together on the ride to Florence in the open Jeep.

We heard the roar of the crowd before we reached the stadium. Troops filled most of seats in the huge stadium. We found seats in the end zone. We forgot about the frosty air when the teams took the field. The atmosphere was equal to a Saturday college football game in the States. A WAC

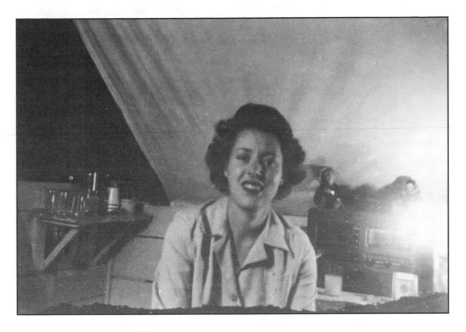

We lined the tent with muslin and added some homey touches

in a skimpy majorette costume led the band in precision marching and college songs at half time. We did not show favoritism and cheered every college rouser. The Fifth Army won the spirited contest. We found our way out of the crowded stadium and went to the officers' club for an evening of dancing. The day was magical and all believed it was a signal the war in Italy would end soon.

On our many outings, we became acquainted with Corporal Drew, Dan and Gordon's driver. When they came down one evening in early January, Gwen asked, "What do you do while you're waiting for us?"

"Sometimes I take a nap," said the corporal. "I talk with other drivers, or go for a walk."

As the evening wore on, I forgot about the corporal waiting for us outside. While I was dancing someone tapped my partner on the shoulder and said, "May I cut in?"

"What are you doing here?" I said when I saw Corporal Drew. "Aren't you afraid you'll get in trouble?" An enlisted man had crashed an officers' dance and I had visions of a crisis.

"I just wanted to dance," said the corporal. We took several turns around the dance floor and none of the officers noticed, or else they chose not to say anything.

"Thanks for the dance," he said. "It was worth taking a chance for it."

I stood alone in the middle of the floor and watched him push through the crowd to the exit. He was waiting in the Jeep when the dance was over.

Winter evenings were long and we tried our culinary skills in ingenious ways. We made fudge with sugar, powdered milk, and dehydrated Hershey bars in a gallon can. We boiled the mixture until the bubbles snapped and turned inward. This did not assure perfect results and we often ate the sugary candy with a spoon. We also brewed coffee in a gallon can on the top of the potbelly stove. The coffee was done when the grounds turned over and fell to the bottom of the pot. We tried to make toasted cheese sandwiches by placing them on the stove, but the bread usually burned black before the artificial butter and processed cheese melted. Rations improved in the mess hall and we had fresh eggs once a week.

We achieved a certain degree of comfort in our tents. The days were short and I was content to stay near camp. A leave in Rome didn't have the appeal it had a year earlier. Captain Meadors surprised me early in January when she said, "You haven't had a leave for a while. I'm sending you, Gwen, and a couple of others to the hotel in Rome for a few days."

When I saw Gwen, I said, "I'd rather stay here, but I suppose we'd better go."

"It could be fun," she said. "A few days in a building might be good for us."

The ride to Rome was long and over mountains where the chill winter air permeated every fiber of our bodies.

Like all the army rest hotels, the rooms, service, and food were a treat, and we adjusted to these luxuries quickly. Finding something to do in Rome on winter days was another story. Darkness came early. Italian civilians crowded the streets and we saw few American soldiers. Meals were the highlight of the trip because we did not venture out at night. The damp air was thick with smoke from charcoal burners and Italian cigarettes. We longed to be back in the chill, fresh air at the foot of the Apennines.

We were gone five days and it was finally time to return to camp. We packed and waited in the lobby for our driver to take us back to Scarperia. We bundled in blankets because the open command car offered little protection from the freezing temperature. We realized, after traveling four hours, that we would not reach camp until long after mealtime and everyone was hungry. We spotted a sign on a cliff above the road that said "Tuna" in English.

"I'll go see what they have," said our driver. He ran up the steep stairs to the restaurant.

"They have enough for five servings and want twenty dollars a serving," he said when he returned about twenty minutes later.

We searched our purses and found $120, even though we knew this was an exorbitant price for the food. We didn't have anything to drink and the fish was dry.

When we reached camp and stretched our aching bodies, everyone agreed that "home" had never looked so good. We didn't want another leave until warmer weather.

We followed the news, and it was clear we would not win the war in Italy. The Battle of the Bulge raged on and Italy was the "forgotten front." Supplies came through regularly, but the fighting in Italy got little attention in the news at home. Colonel Blesse received orders to return to the States, adding to our feelings of abandonment. Colonel Ernst replaced him and was a popular choice because of his warm and relaxed manner.

Infantry soldiers sat in cold, lonely foxholes on the mountaintops for days at a time.

I was lying on my cot for a much-needed nap when I heard my name paged. While I walked to headquarters, I wondered who was waiting there for me. It was Leo Eide, an infantryman from home.

"Let's go to my tent and catch up on the news," I said. "What do you hear from the folks back in Williams?"

"We just came back from the front for a few days rest," said Leo. "The mail hasn't caught up with us, so I don't know much."

We were in the tent a few minutes when I remembered the bottle of Seagrams in the pocket of my bedroll.

"I've got something for you," I said.

An astonished look crossed Leo's face. "Oh, thanks, many thanks," he said. "I'd better get back to my outfit." He left abruptly.

He told me later that he ran all the way back to camp shouting, "See what I've got! Didn't I tell you that she's a good friend?" Leo and his buddies had a party and enjoyed a brief respite from the war.

While the fighting slowed during the winter, Italian civilians made some progress in a return to normal life. Among these efforts was a revival of the opera season. Major Nelson, the doctor in charge of my ward, was an opera fan. He got tickets each week for anyone who wanted to go to the opera on Saturday. I went to *Tosca*, *La Bohème*, *La Traviata*, and *La Forza del Destino*. The small opera house, the Verdi, was in the heart of the city and was surrounded by ancient buildings. Our box seats, richly furnished with gold gilt, red velvet, and dark mahogany wood, were on the first tier. Italian civilians filled every seat on the main floor. They immersed themselves in the music and many mouthed the words to the entire libretto. I found watching them as entertaining as the opera on stage. I wondered how long before their lives and country would be completely normal.

I received a promotion to First Lieutenant just before my twenty-sixth birthday on March 17, 1945. I marked three years in the service on that date by sewing three gold bars on the sleeve of my uniform. Friends showered me with silver bars to replace the gold ones of a Second Lieutenant. With the promotion came a raise in pay to $125 a month.

I was charting a few days later and heard the tent flap at the end of the ward open. I blinked to see more clearly as the figure approached. It was Jon.

"I didn't expect to see you," I said, afraid he would hear my racing heart. "When did you get back?"

"We landed in Rome yesterday," said Jon, "and I didn't expect to see the hospital still here."

"Didn't you hate to come here again?" I asked.

"Not really," said Jon. "I was anxious to get back. It's not the same in the States with the war still going on."

When I saw Lena a few days later, she said, "Jon and Whitey want us to join them for a little party to celebrate Jon's return. We're supposed to meet them by the front gate at 1900 hours."

They led us through the dark to a small Italian home in the village of Scarperia. Whitey tapped on the door. A short, plump Italian woman, about fifty and dressed in black, slowly opened the door. When she saw who it was, a broad smile crossed her face and she gestured for us to come in.

A small table set with four places was a few feet from the fireplace. Candles and a crackling fire were the only source of light in the dimly lit room. An alabaster box carved by Whitey, a talented artist and cartoonist, along with a bottle of Coca-Cola, was by each plate. The heavy aroma of garlic and Italian herbs filled the small room. The woman disappeared behind a curtained doorway. She came back a few moments later with a tray loaded with two roasted chickens, small browned potatoes, carrots, and zucchini.

A bottle of fine Italian wine accompanied the meal. She beamed broadly when we exclaimed about the feast set before us.

"Where did you get the Coke?" I exclaimed.

"How did you find this woman?" said Lena. "I've never eaten such wonderful food."

"We have our ways," said Jon slyly.

"I'll always remember this wonderful meal," I said. It was my first time in an Italian home and that made the evening even more memorable.

We found our way home in the darkness and Whitey answered the challenge of the guard at the gate with the password for the day.

The days wore on and the troops prepared once more to cross the Apennines into the Po Valley. The Allies broke through the German defenses in Europe and the prospects for the end of the war appeared hopeful.

The air was damp and chilly on April 12, 1945. I was standing by the stove to warm myself and make coffee when Danny came through the tent flap. Her face was ghostly white except for her dark freckles.

"What's the matter?" I asked anxiously.

"Haven't you heard the news?" she said, and before I could answer, she said, "Roosevelt died!"

"No! No! Are you sure?" I said. "We just elected him again."

"Oh, Avis, what are we going to do?" cried Danny.

Shocked and grieved, I said, "We'll never get home now."

"And to think we'll have that fool Truman for president," said Danny, a thought that had not crossed my mind.

We cried and shared our grief over the devastating news. How would the death of our president affect us? We marked our second anniversary overseas a few days later, but no one felt like celebrating. The official thirty days of mourning were not long enough.

Fierce fighting on the continent continued. Preparations for the spring offensive in Italy accelerated. The pain of President Roosevelt's death eased. The main objective was still the defeat of Germany.

We greeted each day with a mixture of impatience and apprehension. The days were longer and the snow receded farther up the mountainsides every day. We expected the push into the Po Valley to start when conditions were right.

Rita, the other nurse on the ward, said, "Bob's outfit is giving a party tomorrow night. They would love for some of us to come."

"I think I'll skip this party," I said. "I've been to three in the past four days."

"Oh, please come," said Rita. "They're on alert and who knows what will happen in a few days."

"I'll think about it," I promised.

"You won't have to dress up. They found a barn and are having the party in the haymow."

I cleaned the mud from my boots and wore a freshly laundered shirt and pants. I felt underdressed for a party. It was dark when we arrived at the stone barn and climbed the steep stairs. The haymow was clean and the floor glistened in the candlelight. A record player blared the latest tunes and many men wanted to dance. I soon forgot I wore combat boots as we glided across the slippery floor. Those not dancing gathered around the bar in a corner of the haymow. I sensed their somber mood under the forced gaiety.

I was leading the way downstairs when the party was over. We groped our way in pitch darkness. Near the bottom, I stepped on something that moved.

"Oh, my gosh! What was that?" I screamed.

Hogs slept at the foot of the stairs. Squeals and grunts clearly showed that I had disturbed their sleep. The war disrupted the lives of animals, too.

The men, especially infantry, were in our thoughts and prayers in the tension-filled days ahead. Our six-hole latrine was a popular place to hear current rumors about when the big offensive would start. A common greeting was, "What's the latest Latrine-o-gram?"

The answer to that question came on April 16, 1945. The sky north of us glowed like a setting sun at 2000 hours. The rumble of guns shook the ground. The offensive started and we prayed it would be the final battle in Italy.

Bologna fell to the Allied troops. Orders came for us to move four days after the offensive started. Next came the monumental task of packing our belongings. We parted with ration boxes and other contraptions we had gathered the past seven months to make ourselves comfortable. Italians circled the perimeter of the camp eyeing these treasures and eagerly awaited our departure.

Reveille blasted throughout camp at 0500. The men finally loaded the last piece of equipment about noon. No one minded the wait because we were certain this was the last move for the hospital. Everyone expected to be on their way home soon.

The brilliant sunshine warmed us in protected areas, but the mountain air still had a winter chill. The open trucks offered little protection, so everyone needed extra clothing. We sang "Over hill, over dale, as we hit the dusty trail" with more gusto than at any time before.

The convoy slowly climbed higher and higher over narrow mountain roads. We became even more aware of the brutal fighting that had taken place here the past few months. Shell holes pockmarked every square foot of the mountainsides. Piles of rubble marked the location of former homes. Wrecked German and Allied vehicles along with wooden ammunition boxes littered the roadside. Dust-covered bodies barely off the roadside added to the ghastly scene. I felt a profound inner sadness and realized even more that it was hell on earth for the men fighting here. In peacetime, it was a setting unsurpassed for beauty.

The convoy stopped when we neared the summit of the pass. The stench of rotting flesh nearly overcame us. Two dead horses, with their packs still strapped to their bloated bodies, lay a few feet off the roadside.

We pounded on the truck cab and shouted, "Get this convoy moving! You stopped our truck by dead horses!" The convoy moved slowly forward after twenty minutes.

We saw the broad expanse of the green Po Valley when we reached the summit. The Po River snaked its way through the middle of the valley. The city of Bologna sat pristinely in front of us.

Hospital setup in Mussolini Stadium in Bologna

Chapter XVII

Bologna

When we descended the other side of the mountains, we met an American soldier leading a column of seventy German prisoners. Their dust-covered, sagging bodies belied their age. We guessed many were teenagers. The men did not look like the "superior race." We forgot momentarily that they were the enemy. Truckloads of men, supplies, and armored vehicles in convoy clogged the roads. Scorched, wrecked tanks, artillery guns, and trucks littered the landscape. The devastation was equal to what we saw south of Rome a year earlier.

We wound slowly through the ancient, arcaded streets of Bologna. Throngs of arm-waving, shouting Italian civilians surrounded our trucks. A group of men circled eight women with shaven heads. Found guilty of collaborating with the Germans, they received punishment at the hands of partisans. Was the war over? The chaotic scene indicated that the German forces were disintegrating. I sat quietly and watched events unfold around us. I was afraid to speak for fear the magic moments would evaporate.

The convoy entered a stadium that was our hospital site. We quickly set up cots for the night. Everyone was tired and dirty. The red crosses, marking the stadium as a hospital, could wait until morning. We didn't feel them necessary because we hadn't heard from the Luftwaffe in several weeks. It became clear with each passing hour that the Germans were on the run.

"I'm going to fill my canteen because I can't go to sleep until I wash my face," I said to Mary.

I was about fifty yards from the tent when I heard red alert. The familiar sound of chugging engines told me that German planes were overhead. Where could I run? We did not have foxholes or air-raid shelters. I dashed toward the bleachers in the stadium. I dropped to the ground and pressed tightly against the lowest row of seats. I found I still had the Anzio Shakes during a raid. I shook violently while the planes made pass after pass overhead unloading their deadly cargo. I prayed, "Dear God, don't they know they've lost the war?" I took a short painful breath after each screeching bomb fell outside the stadium. After an hour, the large concentration of troops and antiaircraft guns in the area chased the planes away. I returned to the tent without the water. It was no longer important to wash my face.

After a short night of exhausted sleep, we awoke to bright sunshine on April 25, 1945. We set up the hospital, hopefully for the last time. Allied casualties were very light, but unguarded German ambulances brought wounded by the hundreds. The drivers took their patients to the receiving tent. Then they turned themselves and the vehicles in at our motor pool. German doctors and corpsmen worked alongside our personnel caring for their sick and wounded.

Long lines of German troops marched south in groups, rather than columns. It was clear that their once-organized army had disintegrated. Allied troops surrounded Milan on the south and east and it was impossible to identify the front.

Everyone who ventured outside the stadium came back with a different rumor. We heard of the execution of German collaborators. Some saw Mussolini's body hanging in a square in Milan. The Allies blocked the Brenner Pass and the fighting was all but over in Italy.

"Let's go for a walk," I said to Danny. "All these rumors are getting to be too much."

"We can't go far," said Danny. "It's too dangerous because of snipers and most places are off limits."

"Let's climb to the top of the bleachers. We should get a good view from there," I said. "I'd like to get a closer look at that statue."

The handsome piece of art was a statue of Mussolini astride a horse. Partisans cut El Duce from his steed with a blowtorch after Bologna fell. Only the horse and Mussolini's legs remained. We had a panoramic view of Bologna and the surrounding countryside from the top of the stadium. A lush, flat, green valley surrounded the city. The climb was a favorite form of exercise in the next few days. I found it a refreshing place for contemplation and reflection.

A cemetery a short distance from the stadium also became a favorite place to visit in the long, balmy spring evenings. The graves dated back to ancient times. The cemetery held more than seven million graves on seven underground levels. Wandering through the grounds equaled a visit to an art museum. We saw an astonishing display of statuary. Death was depicted by angels, cherubs, and doves. Each grave was different. Statues of the Virgin Mary, Jesus, the Pietà, and weeping mourners were popular. Clumps of yellow daffodils, purple violets, and red tulips lined the paths between the graves. Danny and I were sorry when the sun went down and we had to return to camp.

Rumors flourished and word that Germany had surrendered passed through the camp almost hourly. Friends from early days in Africa came by to bring us up to date on the front. Their reports added to the speculation that the war was all but over in Italy. We received orders on the morning of April 30 to move the hospital to Milan. We were many miles behind the troops. The orders were cancelled later in the day. We understood the confusion at Army headquarters. We waited patiently for official word that the war was over.

I met Captain Bradley, one of our doctors and a special friend, on my way to the mess hall the following day.

"Hi! I was looking for you," he said. "Did you hear about the 'liberation' made by the 88th Division?"

"I've heard so many rumors, I don't know what to believe," I said. "What's this one about?"

"This isn't a rumor," said Sam. "They found a cave near Brenner Pass full of every conceivable kind of liquor."

"They should give a party for the whole Fifth Army," I said.

"Two of the officers brought a Jeep-load for us," he said. "We're having a party tonight. I'll come by for you after supper if you'd like to go."

We heard the laughing and shouting before we reached the mess hall tent. Tubs, kettles, pails, and even a few helmets were full of ice and dozens of bottles of champagne. Someone handed me a bottle. I turned it over and read the label, which said "Good American Champagne." No one bothered with glasses; we all just drank the heady stuff from the bottle.

"The krauts were probably saving this stuff for their victory celebration," said someone.

"That's the reason I like it even more," said someone else.

"They don't have much to celebrate anymore," chimed in another.

Events moved rapidly in the next few days. We received the word calmly on May 2, 1945, that hostilities in Italy and parts of Austria had ceased. I thanked God I had survived. I grieved for those that hadn't and prayed for an end to war everywhere soon. Our troops were still fighting in Belgium, Holland, and Germany. Berlin fell in the next few days. Hitler and his mistress,

Eva Braun, committed suicide. The Russians marched through Germany. President Truman announced to Congress on May 9 that Germany had accepted an unconditional surrender. The war in Europe was over.

The end of fighting was hard to comprehend. The steady stream of broken, wounded, and dying coming to the hospital ended. We no longer listened for throbbing engines of enemy planes overhead. There was no need for a blackout, so we rolled up the tent sides and turned on every light. The sound of gunfire and crashing shells was over. Even the weight of heavy helmets was lifted from our weary heads. But the fighting with Japan raged on, and that had a sobering effect on our victory celebration.

We had an opportunity to explore the countryside after hostilities ceased. I met Capt. Bill Cooper from Des Moines at a party and he asked, "How would you like to go to Milan tomorrow?"

"I'd like to see Milan," I said. "May I ask my friend Danny to go with us?"

"Sure," he said. "I'll come by in the middle of the morning."

When I saw Danny, she said, "I'm sorry but I've already made plans."

"I hate to go alone," I said. "I don't know him very well, but I know many of his friends."

"You'll be fine," Danny said reassuringly. "Didn't you say he's from Des Moines?"

Captain Cooper had a driver. We sat in the back of the command car and enjoyed the beautiful countryside of grape arbors and broad, green fields. This part of Italy was serene and peaceful, unlike other parts of the country.

Milan suffered little damage from the war. We strolled under the arcades that covered the sidewalks and stopped at an outdoor cafe for a glass of wine. The shops, mostly jewelry stores, had a few pieces of merchandise. I bought a gold filigree bracelet with green stones.

Our next stop was the cathedral that dominates the skyline of Milan. The cathedral is the largest, most beautiful Gothic structure in the world. The roof is surrounded with more than two thousand spires and pinnacles. Each spire and pinnacle is adorned with a statue of an important figure in church history. The tallest spire held a statue of the Virgin Mary. We spent an hour there, but it was not long enough to fully appreciate the beauty of the structure.

In the middle of the afternoon, I said, "Maybe we should go home." The captain's company was beginning to annoy me.

Just after we started back to Bologna, the captain pulled me roughly to him and tried to kiss me.

"Please don't," I said. I set my cap straight and pulled my skirt over my knees.

The situation deteriorated into a wrestling match. I fought off the captain, whose hands were all over me.

"Stop this car!" I shouted to the driver. "Let me out. I'm going to walk home!" We were still about thirty miles from camp.

The driver turned and I sensed a look of pity and sympathy on his face.

"You don't need to get so upset," said the captain.

I glared at him and said, "When I say no, I mean no."

I moved into the farthest corner of the seat and didn't say another word for the rest of the trip. When we reached camp, I jumped from the car. I didn't turn to say good-bye.

I saw Danny the next day and she asked, "How did you like Milan?"

"Milan is beautiful and I wish you'd gone with us," I said ruefully. "The man was a wolf, and that spoiled the trip for me."

We had few patients, so everyone had a five-day leave at a rest camp. The first group of officers and nurses went to Switzerland. This was a special treat because the Swiss had closed their borders during the war. Another group went to Austria and southern Germany. I felt I had an unlucky draw when my orders read "Lake Maggiore at Stresa-Barromea."

I waited eagerly for Danny to return after her trip to Switzerland. "What's it like there?" I asked. "It must be a different world with no war damage. What are the people like?"

"Avis, I've never had so much fun!" exclaimed Danny. "The people were wonderful and so happy to see us." She went on, "We had all the fresh milk we could drink. I've never eaten so much chocolate."

"The group that went to Austria should be back in a few days," I said. "I wonder if they enjoyed their trip."

I saw Sam a few days later, and he said, "You won't believe what's been going on inside Germany. Some of the fellows took pictures and they're developing them in x-ray."

"I'd like to see them," I said. "Did they see Hitler's Eagle's Nest at Berchtesgaden?"

Sam brought the pictures the next day. He said, "I don't know if I should show these to you."

Piles of emaciated, naked bodies, piled like cordwood, horrified and sickened me.

"Where did they get these? Are they pictures of people?" I asked in disbelief.

"They're from a prison camp in southern Germany," said Sam. "George took them between bars in the fence."

We heard about more atrocities each day. It was hard to erase the photo images from my mind.

Our group, which included Sam, left for Lake Maggiore a few days later. It soon became clear that this part of Italy was unlike any we had seen before. Cypress and evergreen trees, along with well-tended formal gardens, surrounded the stone villas that dotted the countryside. Farmers worked the broad fields of corn, oats, and endless grape arbors. Fair-skinned natives were smartly dressed. The small villages did not suffer any damage from the war.

Beyond the farmland, the landscape changed dramatically. We climbed higher and higher as we approached the Alps. Our route took us over hairpin curves and switchbacks that surrounded awesome canyons, high waterfalls, and deep forests. When we could go no higher, our vehicle stopped in front of a breathtakingly beautiful hotel. The structure was a three-story white building with white columns and a canopy over the veranda. The hotel faced an island-studded lake. Carefully pruned shrubs and trees bordered the formal gardens. The lake shimmered in the sunshine. The magnificent, rugged peaks of the Alps served as a backdrop.

I saw Sam alight from one of the vehicles. "Isn't this place beautiful?" he said. "How'd you like to meet me at dinner and go to the dance tonight?"

"I'd love it!" I answered. I was grateful Sam was on the trip. I felt safe with him and appreciated his gentlemanly ways.

Everyone was ready to relax and celebrate. We adapted quickly to the luxurious surroundings, fine meals, and attentive hotel personnel. Doormen opened glass doors at one end of the ballroom to give us a view of the lake. We watched the moon shining on the water while we danced.

We spent our days sitting in chairs on the lawn and talked about our plans when we got home. We explored the lake in paddleboats because the shoreline was filled with big rocks and boulders. An Italian took us to three different islands, where we bought souvenirs. Each of the islands specialized in a form of art, either wood carving, sculpture, painting, or mosaics. I bought three corks with small wood carvings of men attached.

We made a trip to the Swiss border. A guard stopped the train and watched while everyone got off. We looked across the closed border of the country we longed to visit.

Everyone was eager to return to Bologna after five, fun-filled, relaxing days. We expected information telling us when we would return to the States.

On leave at Lake Maggiore

The army devised a plan for rotation home. We received five points for each month of service and five points for each battle. Those with the highest number of points went home first. This was a fair plan. "How many points do you have?" became a common greeting. Most of us had many months of service. We thought our chances of going home soon were very good. We felt it was unfair when the army did not give points for Anzio because the battle was a "strategic failure."

The officer's bugle call sounded over the PA on May 17. Everyone thought, "This is it! Our orders came!" The announcement dashed our hopes. The orders were for us to move to Udine on the Yugoslavian border. There was a dispute between Italians and Marshal Tito's partisans over boundaries. Allied troops were in the area and they needed a hospital. We were angry and disappointed. It was hard to accept the possibility that we might be involved in another war.

Chapter XVIII

Udine

It was a disheartened group that started the long trip north to Udine. We felt that the army had forgotten us. The assignment to open another hospital was difficult to accept.

We tried to get our songfest started. "Let's forget it," said someone. "I don't feel like singing." Everyone agreed that we weren't in the mood to sing.

The convoy wound northward across the Po River. We drove through Padua and close enough to Venice to catch a glimpse of the city in the distance. It was early evening when we reached the hospital site. It took nine hours to make the 225-mile trip. I was stiff and my legs were numb from sitting on the slat benches. Twelve of us shared a truck bed and we had little room to stretch our legs. Three soldiers came to help us to the ground and I gladly accepted their assistance.

Six nurses shared a pyramidal tent for the night. We didn't worry about German planes overhead to disturb our sleep. Canvas cots never felt so good.

A night's rest revived us. The morning was bright and warm, so we set out to explore our surroundings. Broad, flat meadows separated the hospital, service units, and our living quarters. We took advantage of the large area assigned to the hospital and used the space freely. Julian Alps on the east and Carnac Mountains to the north belonged to the broader Dolomite range, the most beautiful mountains in Italy. The rugged peaks formed a spectacular backdrop for the wide, flowering fields, quaint villages, and flat landscape. Venice was a two-hour drive to the southwest. Trieste, on the Yugoslavian border, was an hour southeast of us.

The atmosphere in the area was tense, so we stayed close to camp. Yugoslavian and Italian partisans, armed with rifles, pistols, and grenades, paraded in the streets of the surrounding villages. Many small towns were off limits, and we found it unsettling.

I went to bed early because I treasured a night of sleep without interruptions. One of the first nights, I heard someone outside the tent call my name. It was about midnight. I opened the tent flap and saw a guard who patrolled the area. He said, "Lieutenant Henny is down by the gate and she is causing quite a disturbance."

"What's she doing there?" I asked.

"The MP found her in a little village near here, and that town is off limits."

I slid on my shoes, threw on a robe, and followed the guard to the gate of the camp.

"We don't want her to get into trouble," he said. "That's why we came to get you."

Mary was lying on the ground, disheveled and without her shoes.

"Come with me, Mary," I said. "We'd better get back to our tent."

"I'm not going!" she shouted. "Go away and leave me alone! I just want to sleep!"

"Maybe we can put her on a cot and carry her back to the tent," said the guard. "I'll get someone to help me."

We had gone a short distance when Mary realized what was happening. "Put me down!" she screamed.

"Be quiet!" I said. "We're in front of Colonel Massey's tent and he'll hear you." Colonel Massey was the executive officer.

"I don't care!" she shouted. My heart almost stopped when she cried out, "Colonel Massey, you old son-of-a-bitch, come out here."

"We have to get back to our post," said one of the men.

"I'll stay with her and she'll sober up eventually," I said.

"We'll come back and check on you," promised the guards. I had visions of all of us getting a court martial.

I sat on the ground and rested my head on the cot. It was 0300 hours and I wanted to be on my cot sleeping. After an hour, Mary fell into a deep sleep and the guards returned. They lifted the cot carefully so they would not disturb her. The moon was bright and we cast eerie shadows along the path to our quarters. I breathed a deep sigh of relief when we were safely inside the tent.

I dropped on my cot, afraid to close my eyes. My heart was still pounding when I heard Mary calmly get up and go to the latrine. She came back shortly and then I fell asleep.

I described the night in detail to Mary the next day. She did not remember any of it and felt ashamed. She did not know why she was in the village. We moved into two-person tents a few days later.

Deployment of the troops started and each day brought news of friends returning to the States. Mary's friend Dick had been gone several weeks and she had not heard from him. Our mail came regularly and I prayed each day she would receive a letter. The lack of communication with Dick contributed to her feelings of insecurity and frequent bouts of drinking.

We set up the wards as usual, but we now rolled up the sides and let the summer breezes cool the tents. We had a ball field, and surrounding installations sent teams to our compound for some spirited contests. Movies were popular, and even the poor ones attracted all the patients. One warm evening, a soldier stayed behind on his cot after the others had left for the movie.

"Aren't you going to the movie ?" I asked. "I heard it's a good one."

"Not tonight," he said. "I've got a pain in my stomach and I don't feel well."

I took his temperature and summoned the ward doctor. The doctor examined him and diagnosed appendicitis. The soldier underwent surgery an hour later. After surgery, the soldier returned to the ward. I checked on him every few minutes until he was awake. His cot was empty when I checked one more time.

"Where's the man that was in this bed?" I asked frantically of those around him.

"Oh, he went to the latrine," said a soldier nonchalantly.

The patient came back shortly and lay on his cot without a complaint. This was one of the first cases I'd seen of early ambulation following abdominal surgery. It proved the strength of the American soldier.

We watched the list of those returning to the States grow each day. Among them were my good friends Jack, Dan, and Jon. I was happy for them but I knew our friendship, like the war, was ending. I missed Jon more than any of the others. I knew I'd never have another friend in the army as faithful.

Dan came to say good-bye. "Remember, I live in Chicago," he said. "If you go through there on your way home, give me a call."

"Yeah, if I ever get home," I said with a tinge of self-pity.

Udine was quiet, but we had new problems in our personal lives. We saw boldness in the Italian civilians that we hadn't seen during the fighting. We had only been in Udine a short time before stories began circulating about a few instances of fearless theft.

Mary's bare cot startled me when I returned to our tent in the middle of the afternoon. Why was everything gone? Was she moving?

"All right, who's trying to play a trick on me?" said Mary when she came into the tent.

"I don't know what you mean," I said. "Your cot was bare when I came in a few minutes ago."

We never found a trace of the bedroll that held Mary's clothing and her personal items. Guards patrolled the area, but Italians watched and stole from us with increasing regularity. I laid my clothing on the foot of my cot when I got home from a party a few evenings later. I discovered the next morning that someone had taken the clothes while I slept. Everyone felt vulnerable to bodily attack. Administration increased the number of guards around the nurses' area after there had been many such incidents.

Someone found an excuse for a party almost daily, because the work load was light. We had a birthday party for one of the officers in the mess hall on June 13. Drinks flowed freely. We danced, laughed, talked, and speculated on our next move.

Suddenly one of the guards burst into the tent and walked directly to Colonel Ernst. The crowd hushed when we saw the stricken look on the colonel's face.

"There's been a terrible accident," he said, and he rushed from the tent.

The party ended abruptly. As the details of the accident started to unfold, they shocked and saddened everyone. About eight enlisted men had taken the water-tanker truck for a ride after an evening of celebrating. Several men rode on top of the tank. The truck went off the road, overturned, and killed our cooks, Milonowitz and Blackie, instantly. Some jumped or were thrown free when the truck plunged into the ditch.

Carl Moon was seriously injured. I cared for Carl the next week. He had broken ribs and struggled for each painful breath. I grieved with him over the loss of his buddies. The accident took an emotional toll on everyone.

Carl's physical condition improved after a week and we sent him to a station hospital in Florence.

The days were hot and long in July 1945. If we couldn't go to the United States, the destination everyone longed for, a trip to Venice was better than staying at the hospital.

When I saw Captain Meadors on July 16, she said, "Six of you girls will have a five-day leave in Venice. Your ride will be at headquarters at 0700 hours day after tomorrow."

Gwen was in the group and we spent much of the next day planning what we would do in Venice.

We caught a few glimpses of the Adriatic Sea on our way south before reaching the outskirts of the city. We transferred from the truck to an army duck for the ride down the Grand Canal. We walked across St. Mark's Square, where gondolas waited to take us to the Lido. The old Italian men, dressed in black, shouted to each other as they motioned for three of us to get in each gondola. They pulled the slim gondolas expertly along the lagoon with single poles that barely caused a ripple in the water. The ride was smooth and soon Venice faded in the distance. An island with two elegant white hotels nestled among the cypress and evergreens appeared before us.

"This is the most gorgeous hotel we've seen yet," I said to Gwen. We crossed a spacious lobby with crystal chandeliers, overstuffed furniture, and walls paneled with rich mahogany wood. An elevator took us to the second floor.

Our rooms had high ceilings, tiled baths, rich linens, and an abundance of mirrors.

"I don't know if I like this or not," said Gwen when she looked in the mirror. "Compared to what I looked like when I left home, it's a shock to see myself."

We soon forgot the mirrors and set about exploring our surroundings. Carefully manicured formal gardens, arbors, and fountains flanked the hotel. A broad expanse of grass led to the water's edge. A flotilla of gondolas moored there took guests to the mainland. The Lido was farthest from the war of any place we saw in Italy. The hotels on the island served as rest camps for other military troops. A continuous party mood had prevailed since the war had ended in Italy.

We took a gondola to the mainland where Venetians eagerly waited to show us the city. The gondolier maneuvered through the canals while we lay back and took in the sights around us. We left the gondola at St. Mark's Square in the heart of Venice and ducked hundreds of pigeons that flew around our heads. The guide asked for ten lira (ten cents) to show us the sights and points of interest. Bronze figures atop the watchtower struck a bell with the time.

The Doge's Palace, home of former Venetian rulers, was beautiful, even though some of its art had been removed for safekeeping. Before it was time to go back to the Lido, we crossed the Bridge of Sighs and peered into a dark, damp dungeon. The dungeon had held prisoners in ancient times.

We returned to Venice each day of our leave. We scoured the Rialto Bridge and all the shops under the arcades around St. Mark's Square for something to buy. Iron grillwork or boards covered the windows of most shops. Even though the Italians had stripped the city of its treasures, we still found it a thrilling place to visit.

Our leave was over and we packed to return to the hospital. I said to Gwen, "We should find out where our next trip takes us when we get back."

"Let's hope it's the States and not Japan," said Gwen.

I looked for Danny as soon as I got back to the hospital. "What happened while we were in Venice?" I asked.

"It's been quiet," she said. "We start pistol practice tomorrow, and that will break the monotony."

"Why do we need to know how to shoot guns?" I asked.

"The most popular rumor says our experience here makes us valuable for duty in the Pacific." When she heard my cry of protest, she said, "Don't worry. We'll get leaves at home before we go to the Pacific."

The answers troubled me. Medical personnel were unarmed and I wondered if that had changed. Firearms training dashed our hopes of returning to the States soon.

Everyone was up early the next morning and reported to a shaded bleacher area near camp. A soldier handed each of us a forty-five-caliber pistol before we took our seats for instructions.

A lieutenant about twenty-two years old stood before the group and held a pistol above his head. "You'll learn how to take this piece apart, clean it, and put it together again," he said.

"Why are they teaching us this?" I murmured to Danny. "I couldn't use a gun if I had to."

"We'll do this in a precise, regulation pattern," the officer continued. He strode back and forth in front of us. "This gun's only purpose is to kill!" he said. I shuddered.

We practiced handling the guns for the next three days. Following our instructions, the lieutenant said, "Wear suitable clothing tomorrow, because we're going to the firing range."

We dressed in coveralls and trucks took us to the range. To make sure we handled the guns safely, a soldier stood by each nurse's side. We fired guns, loaded with live ammunition, at a bulls-eye about fifty yards away. We fired from the standing and kneeling positions. After that, we lay on the dusty ground and fired from the prone position. My soldier attendant dubbed me "Annie Oakley." I was an accurate marksman.

The days of pistol practice broke the monotony in our long wait for orders to return home. Everyone worked irregular hours on the wards because the patient load was light.

I awoke with a severe sore throat the day my turn came for duty. My head throbbed and every bone in my body ached. I dressed and went on duty.

When the ward doctor saw me, he said, "Don't you feel well? Your face looks flushed."

"My throat is terribly sore," I said. My temperature was 103 degrees.

He looked into my throat and said, "You have tonsillitis. You'd better go home to bed."

My throat was well after a few days of sulfa, aspirin, and saline gargle. This was my only illness in the army and I regretted spoiling my record.

We looked forward each day to the arrival of the *Stars and Stripes.* We followed our hero, Sad Sack, and chuckled over Bill Mauldin's cartoons of Willie and Joe. The paper also carried news of the war in the Pacific.

At the firing range

Rumors circulated each day that the hospital would close soon. We expected another evacuation hospital to replace us at Udine. We admitted our last patient on August 4, 1945. As soon as we evacuated the last patient or returned him to duty, the hospital would cease to operate.

The hospital admitted and cared for 73,052 patients in twenty-five months of continuous service on foreign soil. We believed this was a record for an evacuation hospital in either theater of war.

I was on the ward packing supplies in preparation for closing when Danny came into the tent waving a copy of the *Stars and Stripes.*

She exclaimed, "Did you see this! They split the atom! We dropped an atomic bomb on Japan on August 6."

I grabbed the paper and read the blazing headlines: "Atomic Bomb Dropped on Hiroshima."

"Can you imagine?" said Danny. "That's equal to thirty thousand tons of TNT."

"They'll have to give up now," I said. I was unable to grasp the enormity of what I had just read.

"And we won't have to go to the Pacific," said Danny. "There's no reason why we won't get home now."

The United States dropped an atomic bomb on Nagasaki on August 9. We waited for word that Japan had surrendered. A serene calm settled over us because we knew the end of the war was near. On August 14, 1945, the *Stars and Stripes* arrived with four-inch-high headlines: "Peace at Last." President Truman announced to the world that the war was finally over.

The last few days at Udine were busy packing hospital supplies and looking for our last souvenir. Many officers I knew brought guns for me to take home as souvenirs.

"I really don't need any souvenirs," I said. "The memories of the past two and a half years will be enough."

"You can take three guns," said one officer. "Don't you think your dad and brothers would like one?"

I agreed to take a German P-38 and two Italian Berettas. Someone gave me a Nazi flag; it took little space in my luggage. I carried the flag and guns in my hand luggage and they were heavy. I often thought of leaving them behind before I got home.

Orders came for us to move to Montecatini Redeployment Center in preparation for our trip home on August 20, 1945. We received the news calmly.

Chapter XIX

Home

We were up and packed at 0500 hours. The trucks didn't come until 0900 hours. The wait did not surprise us because we expected the army's usual "hurry up and wait." No one minded this time because our move was south instead of north into another battle.

Montecatini is about twenty miles west of Florence. It is about three hundred miles from Udine to Florence. We again crossed the Apennine mountains that run the entire length of the Italian Peninsula.

Montecatini, a small town with seven hundred hotels and spas, is famous for its mineral water. Wealthy Florentines and Romans came before the war to pamper themselves and bathe in the healing waters.

Our quarters were on the second floor of a spa in the center of town. All the nurses shared a large dormitory-type room. While there were some personality clashes, it did provide an opportunity to know some of the women better. We mistakenly believed it would be a short stay before moving to Naples where a ship waited to take us home.

Day after day passed without any word as to when we'd leave Montecatini. I was restless and longed for something to fill the long hours.

"I've got to get in shape," I said to Madge Teague, an anesthetist. "I don't want to go home looking like I've been through a war."

"I do, too," said Madge. "Maybe we can find a place to exercise."

We searched the building and found a dusty room on the floor above us. Each morning Madge and I climbed the stairs and spent the next hour stretching, pulling, and pounding ourselves. Perspiration and dirt covered our tired bodies at the end of the hour.

"Why don't we walk to Montecatini Alto tomorrow instead of exercising?" I asked Madge.

"I'd like to," she said. "This fall weather will be a pleasant change from that dusty room."

Montecatini Alto was a low mountain that stood above our hotel. The group of buildings at the top aroused our curiosity. The summit appeared close but was actually four or more miles away.

We filled our canteens with water but didn't take any food with us on our walk. Both of us believed the exercise and no lunch would get us in shape even faster than calisthenics.

We had gone but a short distance when a Jeep with two officers stopped and asked if we wanted a ride.

"No thanks," we replied. "We need the exercise."

Several more vehicles stopped and we gave the same reply. As the morning wore on, the grade got steeper and the buildings did not appear any closer. There wasn't a vehicle in sight when our legs began to give out.

"Maybe we should go back," I said.

We started down the mountain and were nearly at the bottom when two men offered us a ride, which we gladly accepted. Both Madge and I spent the rest of the day on our cots sleeping. We went back to our exercise routine the next day.

Exploring the town was a popular way to spend the day. There weren't any military targets near Montecatini so it did not suffer war damage. Italians had deserted the town, but signs of an indulgent lifestyle remained. Some of the spas were opulent. One near our quarters was especially beautiful. Tall pink-marble columns and statues of nude women surrounded a round pool in the lobby. Bright sunshine poured through the skylight, and the pool sparkled even though it didn't contain water.

Despite our boredom with so little to do, everyone hesitated to go far from our quarters for fear the orders would come while we were gone. Danny and I went to the airfield one day and caught a plane for a quick trip to Rome. We had no problem getting a ride down and back. Our first stop was at a beauty shop where we each had a manicure. The operators answered with an enthusiastic *"Si! Si!"* when we gestured what we wanted. We spent the rest of our time in the well-stocked PX. Olive-drab or beige regulation rayon dresses and olive-drab slacks were for sale.

"Wouldn't you know?" said Danny. "They've got all these clothes, now that the war is over."

"We can snip the buttons off the dresses when we get home," I said. "I'll wear mine in civilian life."

I bought a brown canvas Val-pak (suit bag) trimmed with leather to carry my new clothes. My footlocker already bulged with clothing. We repacked our bags daily. Everyone was ready for the moment when we would leave Montecatini.

The captain came into the quarters one morning. We thought, *This is it! Our orders came!* Instead, she said, "Everyone is to meet on the drill field, in full uniform on September 15. The Surgeon General is making a presentation to the hospital. You may wear either duty or dress uniform, but no civilian shoes." Mary and I exchanged winks because we knew she had directed the remark at us.

We assembled in formation before a reviewing stand at 1000 hours. An American flag fluttered overhead. Everyone snapped to attention when the general appeared. They saluted, and he then presented the award to Colonel Ernst. The citation read, "The 56th Evacuation Hospital is awarded the Meritorious Service Unit Plaque for superior performance of duty in the accomplishment of exceptionally difficult tasks, from 1 March to 30 April 1945 in Italy. Operating in the Apennine Mountains under severe climatic conditions, members of the 56th Evacuation Hospital consistently displayed the highest devotion to duty in the medical treatment of the sick and wounded. The technical skill and resourceful initiative of this organization during the final Po Valley offensive resulted in saving of countless lives and the alleviation of much suffering. Its accomplishments reflect great credit to the Medical Department of the Army of the United States."

This was the last time all hospital personnel gathered in one group. I looked up and down the columns. The thought struck me that I would never see many of these people again.

The orders to proceed to Naples arrived on September 19, 1945. I spent the next day repacking my bags. The army took care of large bags. We carried our helmets, musette bags, canteens, and mess kits along with the hand luggage that held the guns.

"I'm tempted to ditch these guns because they're so heavy," I said to Mary.

"You've carried them this far," she said. "I'd figure out some way to get them home."

"Maybe some day I'll think of them as good souvenirs," I said. "Right now, I don't."

We made the trip to Naples by C-47 instead of truck. That was a pleasant surprise! We flew high enough that we saw no signs of war damage. Italy with her majestic mountains, broad fields, and vineyards looked peaceful.

The trip took only two and a half hours. Everyone rejoiced that the army had spared us a two-day trip by truck.

Trucks met us at the airfield. We were sure we would go directly to a ship waiting in the harbor. Even after several years, we had not learned that the army does not operate that way.

Our quarters were in a former government building a short distance from the harbor. All the nurses were in one large room. The cots were crowded tightly together, about two feet apart. We stuffed our belongings under our cots and waited. Everyone believed we would leave soon, although no date was set.

We spent the next few days near our cots. We didn't want to waste time when word came that the ship was ready. Danny and I spent hours playing gin rummy, and she won every game.

"Are you going to stay in the army?" asked Danny. "I understand we'll all get a chance."

"The idea doesn't appeal to me. I'm ready to make decisions for myself. I've had enough regimentation after three years in nurses' training and almost four years in the army."

"I feel that way, too," said Danny. "I'll probably look for a job in the hospital at home."

"I don't want to do general duty in a hospital," I said. "I'm afraid I wouldn't be patient with someone who came to the hospital for a rest. I've seen too much the past two and a half years."

"Maybe we should take advantage of the GI Bill," said Danny, "and go back to school."

"I'm going to, but I haven't decided what I'll study," I said. "My fantasy is to attend Northwestern and eventually medical school. With all the men returning, and being a woman, I don't have a chance."

"I'd like to get married," said Danny. "The man I want to marry lives in New Jersey. It won't work out because we can't carry on a courtship over that distance."

"Bill will get back from Scotland about the time I get home," I said. "He's too old. We have the same birthday, but he's ten years older than I am."

"That's not too old," said Danny.

"Truthfully, the idea of settling on a farm in Iowa bothers me more. I wouldn't be happy there."

"We'll be able to figure out our lives when we get home," said Danny, always the optimist.

The Italians in Naples were the boldest we'd seen anywhere, and that was even more reason to stay close to quarters. An Italian snatched a purse from one of the nurses just outside our building. The thief ran into a crowd and other Italians helped him escape.

A nurse who dared venture out came back and announced, "Our ship is tied up at the dock. It's the *Vulcania,* a former Italian luxury liner. Of course, it hasn't sailed in many months, so they're refurbishing and fitting it for troops."

A couple of days later someone came to the quarters with the report, "They're scraping the barnacles off. When that's done, we'll be ready to leave."

The ship was finally ready and we took our last truck ride to the dock for loading on September 24. The *Vulcania* was resplendent, with lights blazing from every deck. The Stars and Stripes flew from the highest mast. Five thousand troops squeezed into every inch of space on the ship, but no one minded the crowding. We stayed in the harbor overnight and sailed the next morning. We had landed in Italy two years earlier.

Small tugboats eased the *Vulcania* away from the dock on September 25, 1945. They skillfully maneuvered the huge ship past wreckage that still filled the harbor. When we passed the Isle of Capri, the coastline of Italy faded into the distance.

We moved freely about on the ship. Regulations about fraternizing with enlisted personnel all but disappeared. Card games started as soon as we were in open water. Officers, enlisted men, and nurses sat in circles on the deck for rummy, pinochle, and hearts. When more joined the game, we added another deck of cards. Fire and abandon-ship drills started immediately. We took these exercises seriously because there wasn't any restriction on smoking and almost

Lt. Mary Henehan with Vulcania in background

everyone smoked. Lavish mahogany trim decorated each wooden deck.

When dusk fell, lights flooded the decks and superstructure of the ship. I thought about the danger that had surrounded our trip in total darkness in April 1942. I went alone to an open space along the rail. I again thanked God I had survived.

I saw Mary standing alone a few feet away. "I met one of the crew and he said we'd pass Gibraltar tonight," said Mary. "We don't want to miss it."

It was cloudy when we went to the upper deck about midnight. On the port side was "the rock" ablaze with lights, like a huge birthday cake. Total darkness had shrouded Gibraltar for so long. Lights from the coastline of Spain flickered on the starboard side. The ship sailed through the straits. The door finally opened and we were free to go home.

We had been at sea five days when I said to Danny, "The moon is bright. Let's go to the upper deck. I want to get out of this crowded stateroom for a while." The full moon cast a bright path on the calm water. The light disappeared on the horizon. Like my life, the road ahead looked bright, but I couldn't see where it led.

"We should be in New York in a few days," said Danny. "I think I'll have enough travel by the time I get home."

"I'm going to Seattle and visit my brother, Dorian, who's in the navy," I said. "Leona and her new husband live there, too. Above all, I want to be home for Christmas."

"We'll probably need to go shopping," said Danny.

"I can hardly wait," I said. "I'm going to Des Moines and get a whole new wardrobe. My first stop will be Cownie Furs to buy the most beautiful fur coat I can afford. I don't ever want be cold again."

After we had been at sea eight days, word reached us that we would be in New York by nightfall. We dressed casually for the crossing and now everyone crowded the stateroom to change into the required dress uniform. We deserted the mess hall for the evening meal. No one wanted to miss the first glimpse of United States. We strained our eyes scanning the horizon for any irregularity on the endless sea. Ever so slowly, something appeared. When it became clear that it was indeed land, the murmurs turned into a roar.

The ship glided smoothly along the coastline before turning up the channel of the East River. Everyone aboard crowded the decks for the best possible view. We shouted to hands on the decks of smaller boats in the river. We did not expect answers to the din of questions; we just wanted to hear someone from home speak to us.

We heard American music that grew steadily louder as the ship moved along. We rushed to the starboard side. A small boat gaily decorated in red, white, and blue bunting came into view. A lively combo of accordion, banjo, and trumpet played "Sentimental Journey," "My Dreams Are Getting Better All the Time," and "Beer Barrel Polka." They waved and shouted, "Welcome back! We're glad you're home."

My throat was tight and I could speak only in a whisper. Tears streamed without shame down every face on board the ship.

"The Statue of Liberty is coming up on the port side!"

We stampeded to the port side. Everyone crowded the rail, causing the boat to list until it almost capsized. At first, a few light-colored balloons floated skyward. The sky filled with thousands when the Statue of Liberty came into view. Soldiers had filled their GI condoms and sent them aloft as one more way to release their emotions.

Dusk was falling rapidly and lights began to blink when we glided slowly into harbor. We had been briefed on debarkation procedure a few days earlier. We prepared ourselves to wait until our turn came to go ashore. After waiting impatiently, we saw our enlisted men leave the boat. This signaled that debarkation had finally reached the 56th Evac.

A captain on board ship called each name. We filed down the gangplank to set foot on United States soil for the first time in two and a half years. A welcoming committee offered cartons of fresh milk and doughnuts. Some talked, others cried or shouted. I tried to find my own place in the chaotic excitement that surrounded me. We marveled at things we had always taken for granted. Everyone spoke English. Lighted skyscrapers dazzled us. There were American bills and coins instead of French francs and Italian lira. The exhilaration of being in the "land of the free" almost overwhelmed me.

Buses waited along the dock to take us to Grand Central Station. Trains were ready to take us to Ft. Sheridan, Illinois, for our discharge. Even the bus, with upholstered seats and windows that could be raised and lowered, thrilled us.

It was late when we reached the station and walked down the platform to the Pullman cars waiting on the tracks. We traveled across the low mountains of Pennsylvania, the plains of Ohio, and past Cleveland during the night. Everywhere were sights we had forgotten: cars, trains, skyscrapers, small-town depots, and cornfields.

We went to the dining car for breakfast. Orange juice and bananas, only a memory for so long, were on the menu. I no longer feared any problems with adjustment to civilian life. Each ordinary experience pushed the extraordinary of the past two and a half years further back in my mind.

Our route passed the smokestacks of Gary and Hammond, Indiana, and we knew Chicago was the next stop. The train arrived at Union Station shortly after noon on October 3. We boarded buses for the ride to Fort Sheridan, north of Chicago. The skyscrapers on the skyline to the west and Lake Michigan on the east were familiar sights. We reached the post, after many starts and much waiting, in the early evening.

Everyone had an opportunity to make phone calls. My parents did not have a telephone, so I called my sister, Phyllis. She was in Nurses' Training at Iowa Methodist Hospital in Des Moines, Iowa. After the phone rang, I heard someone shout, "Dagit, you have a phone call."

I took a deep breath to collect my composure. When I heard her voice, I started to cry and was unable to say anything. After a few minutes, I said through the tears, "I'm back. How is everyone?"

"We're fine and so happy you're finally home."

The rush of emotions overwhelmed me. "Tell the folks I'll be home on the train Friday morning." I hung up the receiver without saying "good-bye."

We assembled for our assignment of quarters for the night. We reported the next morning for mustering out of the service. We gathered in a barracks that had recently served as an assembly hall for enlisted personnel. Officers and their clerks sat behind makeshift desks in the front of the hall.

"I hate to part with this helmet," I said to Mary. "It's been such an important item in our lives for so long."

An officer called my name. I approached his desk. He pointed to a pile of equipment and I added my musette bag, mess kit, canteen, and helmet. The captain asked a few questions and I answered them to his satisfaction. I was on leave and paid until February 26, 1946. He handed me a gold discharge tack pin in the form of an eagle. The soldiers nicknamed the pin a "ruptured duck" and it was a symbol everyone sought. I received an honorable discharge and a release from active duty in the army. I was free to leave.

The discharge brought an abrupt end to my tour of duty. A part of me felt empty and uncertain of the future. I looked at my friends around me and knew everyone was dealing with the same conflicting emotions.

Danny and I embraced and promised we would keep in touch. I also sought Lena, Gwen, and Madge for a warm good-bye.

"Why don't you stay with me tonight at Sam and Helen's?" said Mary. "I'm going to stay in Chicago until I decide where I'll live." Mary had lost both parents while she was in the army. It was clear that her romance with Dick was over. She had more problems on her return to civilian life than most of us.

Sam was Mary's oldest brother and lived on the north side of Chicago. We were up early the next morning to tell about our trip home. Helen made an appointment for me to go to Carson, Pirie, and Scott for a shampoo, set, and manicure. My train for home left Chicago at eleven that evening.

I took the elevated train to the loop for my four-o'clock appointment. When I looked down on the homes below, everything looked normal. Little children played tag and three girls jumped rope. A group of nine- and ten-year-old boys played baseball in a vacant lot. They laughed and shouted. I thought about the children in Africa and Italy. How had the war affected these children? Did they know how lucky they were to live in United States?

"Are you going to call Dan?" asked Mary when I got back to the house. "I'm sure he'd like to hear from you."

When I hesitated, she said, "We're going bowling this evening. Maybe he could meet you there."

I called Dan, gave him the address of the bowling alley, and arranged to meet him there. We were at the bowling alley when Dan came in, stopped, and looked around before he saw me. He carried a briefcase and wore a long woolen topcoat. It was a dramatic change from the captain's uniform of a few months ago. We hugged and he said, "You look great, not like someone who's been in a war." I concluded that the beautician at Carson, Pirie, and Scott had done a good job.

"It's noisy in here," said Dan. "Let's go someplace where we can talk."

I told Mary good-bye and thanked Sam and Helen. We took my bags, hailed a cab, and went to the Congress Hotel dining room. As we entered, Ray Pearl's orchestra was playing, "You'd Be So Nice to Come Home To." I ordered a glass of wine and Dan had scotch and water.

"How do you like being a civilian again?" I asked Dan.

"It was tough at first," he said. "Everything moves so fast."

"It's a bit scary," I said. "I hope it won't take too long to get used to the pace."

"You'll be fine," said Dan.

The time flew. When I looked at my watch, I said, "Oh, I have to go. My train leaves in forty-five minutes."

We left abruptly, hailed a cab, and made a dash for Union Station. I ran down the stairs and saw the brakeman prepare the train for departure. The conductor shouted, "All aboard," when I was few steps away. He grabbed my hand and pulled me up the steps. Dan threw my bags on the platform between the cars. I ran to a window and waved good-bye to Dan as we moved slowly out of the station. Weak and trembling, I realized that I had almost missed the train for a trip I had waited so long to make.

I sank back in the seat and tried to imagine the future. What would I do now? I was no longer a naive young woman from a farm in Iowa. I had seen war at its worst and survived.

I tried to stay awake, but the rocking of the train and fatigue soon overtook me. I roused briefly when the train stopped in Rock Island and Moline. I knew we entered Iowa there. By the time we reached Independence, the sun was coming up and farmers were in the field harvesting corn. I knew Dad and the boys would not let anything interfere with work on this beautiful fall morning.

"When will we get to Williams?" I asked the conductor.

"We make a brief stop in Iowa Falls and should be there in about an hour," he said.

I searched for a familiar landmark or face in Iowa Falls but didn't see any. When we slowed for Alden, I stood between the cars. Williams did not have a depot and I wanted to be ready when the train stopped. The train braked for Williams. I glimpsed Mother, Edith, Alice, Phyllis, and Elsie standing in the morning sun. I leaped from the train when it stopped and ran to Mother's outstretched arms. The conductor placed my bags alongside the tracks. The war was finally over for me. I was home.

To order additional copies of this book,
please send full amount plus $4.00 for
postage and handling for the first book and
50¢ for each additional book.

Send orders to:

Galde Press, Inc.
PO Box 460
Lakeville, Minnesota 55044-0460

Credit card orders call 1–800–777–3454
Phone (952) 891–5991 • Fax (952) 891–6091
Visit our website at http://www.galdepress.com

Write for our free catalog.